This book is dedicated to Benjamin White Jr. (1951- 2005)

Former Sea Shepherd Director and Founder of the Cetacean Freedom Movement

Library of Congress Cataloging-in-Publication Data available upon request

We chose to print this title on paper certified by The Forest Stewardship Council® (FSC®), a global, not-for-profit organization dedicated to the promotion of responsible forest management worldwide

Printed in Hong Kong
GroundSwell Books
an imprint of BPC
PO Box 99
Summertown, TN 38483
888-260-8458
bookpubco.com
ISBN: 978-1-57067-398-6

25 24 23 22 21 20 1 2 3 4 5 6 7 8 9

We would like to thank PETA for donating several photos - visit www.peta.org

Thank you Celine Tremblay for creating the cover, back, tombstones, and map. Celine has been a Sea Shepherd volunteer since 2010

Thank you Georgina Berryman for donating several photos - visit her Instagram @inherentlywild

Thank you to Captain Paul Watson's Facebook fans who donated photos for this project - to those who asked to remain anonymous, we appreciate your courage and hope you continue to be the eyes and ears for whales in captivity

Last, but not least, we would like to thank David Phillips for allowing us to use his photos, including Keiko on the back of the book: International Marine Mammal Project, Earth Island Institute, 2150 Allston Way, Suite 460, Berkeley, California 94704, www.savedolphins.eii.org

FOREWORD by

Captain Paul Watson

Over the last fifty years, humans have kidnapped, imprisoned and made slaves of one of the most intelligent, socially complex, self-aware species on the planet. Orcas – Powerful yet playful apex predators who have never caused any harm to humans in the wild yet have been captured for the sole purpose of entertaining human beings for profit. It is an evil industry that has made billions of dollars and has caused incredible misery and deaths to these magnificent sentient beings. What do you call a trade that captures, imprisons, possesses, and forces others to work for the profit of legalized owners? There is only one word for it – slavery. The capture, imprisonment, possession, and profits made from the suffering of Orcas is by every definition – a slave trade. Stolen and forcefully removed from their family and their pods (tribes), trained, and selectively bred to work for the profit of the owners, transported, abused, their lives shortened, the dead outnumbering the living, traded like commodities, deprived of food to force compliance, and paraded before people for amusement. These are all the hallmarks of a slave trade and it is a very profitable slave trade that includes not only the Orcas but also numerous species of dolphins with prices that greatly exceed the historical value of human slaves.

The purpose of this book is to introduce the public to the inmates of these Orca prisons. They have names given to them by their owners in the same manner that slave owners of the past named their human property. This book documents where these slaves are held, how they are abused, their forced breeding programs and where they were captured or bred. There are presently 56 Orca slaves held in concrete cells. 162 Orcas have died in captivity. These facilities need to be shut down and the inmates moved to large sea pens and rehabilitated to be released into the wild. We need to abolish dolphin slavery and toss the entire industry into the dustbin of history. It is perversely cruel, unnecessary, unethical, inhumane, and a foul disgrace to humanity.

On these pages you will find the relevant information on the inmates, the victims, and the prisons of this contemptible industry.

INTRODUCTION

Marine mammals from the order cetacea include whales, dolphins, and porpoises. Orcinus orca are the largest members of the family Delphinidae although they are commonly referred to as killer whales. Other names used are Orca, blackfish, and grampus. Orcas are odontocetes, meaning they have teeth as opposed to baleen. Although they have a cosmopolitan distribution, their numbers are only around 50,000. Orcas are at the top of their trophic level and have no predators. Their diets range between ecotypes and can include fish, birds, cephalopods, elasmobranchs, and marine mammals such as other whales, porpoises, and sea otters. They eat on average 4% of their body weight each day.

Resident Orcas live in a matrilineal society in which sons remain with their mother (the matriarch) throughout their lives, while daughters may leave in order to form their own matriline. Several matrilines will come together to form a pod and spend time together.

Males can grow up to 32 feet in length and weigh up to 22,000 pounds, while females can grow up to 29 feet in length and weigh 16,000 pounds. Females are reproductive between the ages of 11 and 45 and have a gestation period between fifteen and eighteen months. Orcas are polygynandrous, both males and females having multiple mates throughout a breeding season and they do not interbreed within their own pod. Mating usually in the summer, but can occur during any season. Calves are born tail first between 7 – 8 feet long and weigh an average of 400 pounds. Females give birth around once every five years and will have around three to five calves in their lifetime (take note in Chapter 4 of when the females in captivity are forced to reproduce). Males become sexually mature between 12 - 15 years.

In the wild, females live on average 50 years while males live on average 30 years. The oldest recorded female Orca was J2 (Granny) from the Southern Resident community who was 105 years old when she passed away in the fall of 2016. The oldest recorded male, J1 or Ruffles, lived to around 60 years old. Life spans in captivity are two and a half times shorter than their wild counterparts.

Sexual dimorphism is shown in the pectoral flippers, girths, tail flukes, and dorsal fins in the males, which can grow to six feet tall. The dorsal fin acts like a keel on a sailboat, stabilizing the whale. Orcas can be identified by their saddle patches, the light area behind the dorsal fin, which can be compared to a human fingerprint in that no two are alike.

Orcas use echolocation to locate their prey and their ears are well developed. This highly attuned sense of hearing does not bode well in a small concrete pool of captivity where reverberations from loud music, cheering crowds, construction work, and banging on glass view windows are constantly bombarding the animals.

Different pods have unique dialects, further differentiating Orca ecotypes. Calves are not born with a full set of repertoire sounds, rather they are learned from the adults. Take note in Chapter 4 where each whale originates from and which Orcas they are forced to live with in captivity.

The Southern Residents off the Northwest Pacific Coast of the United States can swim up to 100 miles a day in search of food and can reach speeds up to 32 mph. Take note in Chapter 4 of the pool tank dimensions captive Orcas are forced to live in.

Orca sightings are common along the coasts of the U.S. North Pacific, Argentina, Australia, Norway, east and west coasts of Canada, Antarctica, Galapagos, Europe, Bahamas, New Zealand, and Iceland. Although sightings are rare, one could see them while whale watching in Hawaii as well.

CHAPTER 1: The Beginning

Since the mid 1800's, marine mammals have been caught and imprisoned for entertainment. P.T Barnum displayed dolphins and belugas and in the late 1800's the Brighton Aquarium in England displayed harbor porpoises. By the 1870's whales and dolphins were being captured and sold to parks in the United States and Europe. Marine Studios opened in Florida in 1938 and housed bottlenose dolphins. Marineland of the Pacific opened in 1954 and closed in 1987 when SeaWorld San Diego purchased the park. Miami SeaAquarium opened its doors in 1955 and to this day continues to house an Orca, a lone female named Lolita. In 1946, the International Whaling Commission (IWC) was formed by fifteen whaling nations in order to regulate whaling and maintain whale stocks. Japanese whalers slaughtered 1,178 Orcas between 1954 and 1997 and the Norwegians killed an average of 57 Orcas per year between 1938 and 1980 (~2,394). In the 1950's, the US Navy regularly shot at Orcas for target practice.

A Browning machine gun was installed on a lookout point on the Campbell River, near the northeast side of Vancouver Island, B.C. after local fishing organizations met with the Department of Fisheries to find a solution to stop Orcas from eating *their* salmon. In the end, the Department of Fisheries determined it was too dangerous for passerbys and the gun was never fired.

In 1956, the US Navy was sent to destroy the entire population of Orcas in Iceland (see appendix for newspaper clipping). According to Guardians of the Whales by Obee and Ellis, "...one-quarter of the Orcas caught for aquariums in the 1960s and '70s bore bullet wounds."

The first Orca was captured in 1961. A lone female Orca was spotted near Newport Harbor off the southern tip of California on November 18, 1961. Frank Brocato from Marineland of the Pacific was in charge of collecting the whale for the park's marine mammal collection. Frank and his team captured the whale and drove her to Marineland in Palos Verdes where she was named Wanda. The next day Wanda began to strike the tank walls and convulse. On November 20, 1961 Wanda died after only 42 hours in captivity. In September of 1962, Frank Brocato travelled to Puget Sound, Washington in search of another Orca. His crew came across a male and female inside Haro Strait between Victoria, B.C. and San Juan Island. A lasso was thrown over the female, but the rope got entangled in the boat's propeller. The female called out to the male and both Orcas charged the immobile boat. Frank shot the male one time and the female ten times with a .375 magnum rifle. No one knows the fate of the male whale as it disappeared after being shot. After towing the female carcass back to Bellingham, Washington she was processed and sold as dog food, but not before Frank removed her teeth and kept them as souvenirs.

In 1964, the Vancouver Aquarium commissioned an artist by the name of Samuel Burich to kill an Orca in order to make a life-sized sculpture for an aquarium exhibit. Samuel set up a harpoon gun on Saturna Island, northeast of Victoria, B.C. and waited two months for a pod of whales to swim past the harpoon. On July 16, 1964 a pod swam by the Island and Samuel harpooned a young (~5-7 yr old) Orca. Members of the pod came to the young whale's aid pushing it to the surface to breathe. Samuel shot the whale with his rifle several times, but the whale did not die. Murray Newman, the manager of the Vancouver Aquarium, decided to try and save the whale and so it was towed over sixteen hours back to Vancouver Harbor and placed in a sea pen. The public voted on a name and at the time it was presumed to be female and so Moby Doll was chosen. Moby Doll finally began to eat after fifty-five days in captivity, but unfortunately a month later on October 9, 1964 *he* died. Not until the necropsy did scientists discover that Moby Doll was in fact a male. Moby Doll was the very first Orca ever to be on public display. It was later determined that Moby Doll was a southern resident from the J pod.

In June of 1965, William Lechkobit found two Orcas in his salmon net off the coast of British Columbia. The adult Orca was able to escape the net, but the calf would not follow. A few days later William checked the net to find the calf gone and the adult inside. By this time, word was getting out that fishermen could make a profit selling caught Orcas instead of releasing them and so William sold the Orca to Ted Griffin of the Seattle Marine Aquarium for $8,000. The whale was transferred via floating sea pen to the Seattle Public Aquarium where he was named Namu, after the location where he was caught. A movie about Namu was made and two weeks before the release on July 9, 1966 Namu died from an infection due to the polluted water in his sea pen (see appendix for movie poster). He was held captive for eleven months.

On October 31, 1965 Ted Griffin and Don Goldsberry attempted to capture a female in order to mate with Namu. In the Carr Inlet west of Tacoma, Washington the crew harpooned a Southern Resident female Orca. The mother's calf followed the mother as she was being towed back to Seattle, but along the way the mother drowned. Even though the female calf was too young (3 years old) to mate with Namu, Ted decided to keep her. By combining the name Namu with the word *she*, the female calf would be the first ever Shamu. Ted sold Shamu to SeaWorld San Diego for $75,000 and on December 20, 1965 Shamu was shipped to the California park. On April 19, 1971 SeaWorld secretary Annette Eckis entered the pool with Shamu for a photo shoot. After climbing onto the whale's back, she rode Shamu around the pool one time and then Shamu began to buck. After she was thrown into the water, Shamu grabbed a hold of her leg and pushed her around the pool periodically dunking her just under the water's surface. A trainer swam to Annette and grabbed her but could not get her out of Shamu's mouth. Another trainer held out a pole for Annette to pull herself out of the pool, but Shamu rammed into her again causing her to let go of the pole. Another pole was stretched out and Annette was pulled up to the side of the pool with Shamu still attached to her left calf. A trainer finally persuaded Shamu to release the woman and she was pulled to safety. Annette was rushed to the hospital where it took one hundred stitches to close her wound. Because of this incident, Shamu was moved to SeaWorld's breeding program, as trainers were not allowed back in the water with her. On August 29, 1971 just four months after the incident, Shamu died of pyometra, an infection of the uterus (see appendix for photo).

In August 1970, the largest Orca round up occurred in Penn Cove southeast of the San Juan Islands, Washington. Griffin and Goldsberry were again in charge of the captures. Eighty Southern Resident Orcas were caught in a large purse seine net (see appendix for photo). Seven Orcas were chosen for parks and three babies died in the net. The bellies of the deceased Orcas were slit open and filled with rocks in order to sink the carcasses. The permit allowed for seven Orcas to be taken and the three dead ones would have counted towards that quota. Only one Orca from that capture remains alive in captivity today, a lone female at the Miami Seaquarium named Lolita. Ken Balcomb of the Center for Whale Research estimated that the population of Southern Residents before the captures in the 60's and 70's was 112 and by 1976 there were only 68. By 1991, the population was depleted to 92 individuals; had the captures never taken place, there would have been 135 Orcas. More than fifty Orcas had been taken from the Pacific Northwest by the mid 1970's and sent to aquariums around the world. On the other side of the world, the Soviet Union killed 916 Orcas in the waters off Antarctica between 1979 and 1980. They typically took around twenty-five per whaling season before this massive slaughter.

The U.S. Congress enacted the Marine Mammal Protection Act (MMPA) in 1972 in order to "prevent marine mammal species and population stocks from declining beyond the point where they ceased to be significant functioning elements of the ecosystems of which they are a part." The Marine Mammal Protection Act does not restrict taking marine mammals for public display or the commercial fishing of Orcas for scientific research (see appendix). Under the MMPA the AT1 Transient Orcas are listed as depleted due to the 1989 Exxon Valdez oil spill near Puget Sound, Washington. To learn about the MMPA visit http://www.nmfs.noaa.gov

The U.S. Congress passed the Endangered Species Act (ESA) in 1973 for "the conservation of species that are endangered or threatened throughout all or a significant portion of their range, and the conservation of the ecosystems on which they depend." The ESA is administered by the U.S. Fish and Wildlife Service and the Commerce Department's National Marine Fisheries Service. Under the ESA, the Southern Resident killer whales (J, K and L pods) are listed as endangered. To learn more about the ESA visit http://www.nmfs.noaa.gov

Also in 1973 the Convention on International Trade in Endangered Species (CITES) was adopted to regulate the worldwide commercial trade in wild animal and plant species. The number of member countries as of 2020 is 183. To learn more about CITES visit www.cites.org

Which Agency protects what species in the U.S.?

- Whales, Dolphins, Porpoises, Seals, Sea Lions – The Department of Commerce through the National Marine Fisheries Service
- Walrus, Manatees, Otters, Polar Bears – Department of the Interior through the U.S. Fish and Wildlife Service
- Captive Marine Mammals – Animal and Plant Health Inspection Service, part of the Department of Agriculture

Other countries have also adopted agreements such as New Zealand, which enacted a Marine Mammal Protection Act in 1978 and Australia, which adopted the Whale Protection Act in 1980.

As recent as 2018, Orcas have been hunted for their meat near St. Vincent and the Grenadines (SVG), a small Caribbean island east of Barbados. The island is exempt from the 1986 Global Moratorium on Whaling that was put into place by the IWC. SVG has slaughtered 28 humpback whales (which have been endangered since 1970) between 2000 and 2015. SVG has hunted hundreds of pilot whales, Orcas, porpoises and dolphins annually since the early twentieth century. The IWC does not regulate the killing of smaller cetaceans such as Orcas. On July 12, 2015 four Orcas were killed for their meat, oil and blubber even though Orcas are known to contain high levels of mercury, lead and polychlorinated hydrocarbons (PCBs). Eight Orcas in total were killed in 2015, two of them being pregnant. There is a small export market of the cetacean meat to the nearby island of Barbados. The Argyle International Airport at SVG opened in 2017, which aims to boost tourism to the country lending itself to the possibility of whale watching, scuba diving, and water sports. In 2017, passengers on a touring boat were watching a pod of four Orcas when a hunting boat approached and killed two of the Orcas with a harpoon gun. This incident led Prime Minister Ralph Gonsalves to announce he would introduce legislation to ban the hunting of Orcas, but in 2018, three more Orcas, one male and two females, were killed and he has yet to introduce any such ban.
Sea Shepherd Conservation Society is currently working with local officials to end the barbaric hunt. To volunteer or donate please visit www.seashepherd.org.

May 6, 2016
Orcas hunted in St. Vincent and the Grenadines
Photo courtesy of Sea Shepherd

Harpoon gun being used for whaling
St. Vincent and the Grenadines in 2016
Photo courtesy of Sea Shepherd

Whaling in St. Vincent and the Grenadines
Photo courtesy of Sea Shepherd

July 12, 2015
"blackfish" hunts in St. Vincent and the Grenadines
Photo courtesy of Sea Shepherd

CHAPTER 2: The Famous

Keiko

Kandu V

Tilikum

Calypso & Clovis

Keto

Luna

Miracle

Keiko

Keiko was a male Orca born in Iceland around 1978. In November 1979 Keiko was caught in a herring fishing net off the southeast coast of Iceland, brought to an undisclosed holding tank and named Kago, which means "little boy" in Icelandic. Kago was sold to Marineland Ontario and shipped to the park along with a female Orca named Kiska in 1982. Kago was housed with five other Orcas in Marineland and routinely rammed by the more dominant whales.

After showing signs of weakness from the aggressions, Kago was placed in a small tank indoors where he was kept alone. In February 1985 Kago was sold again for $350,000 and shipped to a Mexico City Amusement Park called Reino Aventura. Kago was renamed Keiko which means "lucky one" in Japanese. Keiko remained at this park from 1985 until 1996. The tank that Keiko shared with dolphins measured 20 feet deep by 90 feet long by 43 feet wide and was kept at 80 F, much warmer than his native waters in Iceland where they average 45 F. Due to the poor conditions of his tank Keiko development bilateral axillary skin lesions. The viral disease called cutaneous papillomaviral-like papillomatosis was the first case documented in an Orca.

SeaWorld at this time was looking to expand its breeding program and contacted Reino Aventura about purchasing Keiko. SeaWorld instead ended up purchasing Tilikum from Sealand since he was a proven breeder. In 1992, Warner Brothers started filming Free Willy in which Keiko starred. SeaWorld and the Miami Seaquarium declined to allow Warner Brothers to film at their parks and so they decided to film at Reino Aventura. The film was released in 1993 followed by public outcry for Keiko's release back to the wild. The executive producers of the film contacted Ken Balcomb and a rehabilitation and reintroduction plan was created for Keiko. He was finally moved to the Oregon Coast Aquarium in 1996 after years of negotiations between Reino Aventura and several groups. After two years in Oregon, Keiko was moved to a floating sea pen in the Westman Islands, Iceland. In 2002 Keiko made a 1,000-mile trek over five weeks towards Norway.

In the winter of 2002, he was moved to Taknes Bay, Norway for fear he would get stuck under frozen ice. Keiko died on December 12, 2003. A necropsy was not performed so it is unclear what the exact cause of death was.

Keiko in Iceland. Photo courtesy of David Phillips, Earth Island Institute

Kandu V

Kandu V was a three old female Orca captured from Icelandic waters in the fall of 1977 and shortly afterwards sent to SeaWorld San Diego. Kandu V spent some time at SeaWorld Ohio between the spring and fall 1980 and 1981. At SeaWorld San Diego in February of 1984 she pinned trainer Joanne Hay to one of the pool walls. In November 1984, she grabbed trainer Georgia Jones' legs. In November 1986, Kandu V pushed trainer Mark Beeler against a wall.

In 1986 Kandu V gave birth to a dead Orca that she sired with Winston. In 1987, Kandu V and Kenau took turns dragging Jonathan Smith to the bottom of the pool. Jonathan ended up with a ruptured kidney and lacerated liver. A few months later, Kandu V landed on trainer Joanne Weber breaking the trainer's neck, causing her permanent damage to her neck muscles.

Kandu V mated with Orky II and in 1988 gave birth to a female named Orkid. On August 21, 1989 Orkid, then eleven months old, was working with an adult female named Corky II. Kandu V (6,000 lbs.) entered the pool and charged Corky II (8,000 lbs.) ramming into her body. Kandu V broke her upper jaw, severed an artery and bled to death for over forty-five minutes in front of thousands of spectators. Orkid remained close to her mother as she bled out, died, and sank to the bottom of the pool. Corky II did not sustain any major injuries.

Corky II and Kandu V were showing signs of tension leading up to the fatal attack. Corky II was captured from the Northern Resident population (A5) in Pender Harbor, B.C. These two female Orcas would never have come in contact in the wild. They were from different parts of the world, spoke different dialects, and had different diets. Some speculate that Corky II gave Orkid too much attention, which might have caused tension between Kandu V and Corky II. Kandu V was about fifteen years old when she died. Orky II also had trainer aggression incidents starting in 1978 when she held trainer Jim Stratton at the bottom of the pool. In November 1987, John Sillick was riding Nootka when Orky II slammed on top of him resulting in six operations following the incident. Jonathan Smith, John Sillick, and Joanne Weber all sued SeaWorld, but as part of the settlement gag orders were put in place.

Kenau and Kandu V
Photo courtesy of Hah

Tilikum

Tilikum (Chinook for "friend") was captured at the age of two in November 1983 off Iceland. He was sent to Sealand of the Pacific where he lived with Nootka IV and Haida II. The two older females would assert their dominance over the male Tilikum and rake him often. At night all three were kept in a small module because the owners were worried that someone might set them free. From 5pm until 7am the three Orcas were kept in a pool measuring 25 feet wide by 30 feet long. This went on for seven years.

On February 21, 1991, trainer Keltie Byrne fell half way into the pool with the three whales. As she was trying to exit the water, Tilikum grabbed her boot and pulled her back in. Witnesses said it was hard to know which whale had her at which time because the water was dark. There was a lot of splashing and after ten minutes Keltie had drowned. It took trainers two hours to retrieve Keltie's body from the three whales that had never seen a trainer in the water before this incident.

Sealand of the Pacific closed it doors in 1992 and sold the three whales to SeaWorld. Tilikum was shipped to SeaWorld Orlando that same year to join its breeding program. Once in Orlando, Tilikum was again displaced by the older females, especially Katina. While in Orlando, the trainers were given a set of rules that only applied to Tilikum, one being that no one was allowed to lie down near the large male. On July 7, 1999 Tilikum was found swimming around his pool with the body of Daniel Dukes draped over his back. Daniel remained hidden in the park the night before and then entered the pool with Tilikum. He was found the next morning dead, naked, covered in bite marks and missing his genitals.

On February 24, 2010 Tilikum pulled trainer Dawn Brancheau into a pool and killed her. Dawn was working with Tilikum during a Dine with Shamu show when she lay down next to him in a shallow part of the pool only inches deep. Tilikum grabbed her arm, pulled her into the pool, and began pushing her around. Tilikum ignored all emergency recalls, but eventually swam into the medical pool and was lifted out of the water, with Dawn still in his mouth. The official autopsy report stated that Dawn suffered from a broken jaw, ribs and sternum, dislocated elbow and knee, fractured neck, was scalped and missing her arm, which was later removed from Tilikum's mouth. Her hair and bridge (the whistle trainers use to reinforce desired behaviors) were found on the bottom of the pool. Dawn died in SeaWorld's "G" pool, the same pool that Daniel Dukes was found dead in 1999. On January 6, 2017 Tilikum passed away from a chronic and progressive bacterial lung infection. He was in captivity for 33 years and sired 21 calves.

November 2014
Photo courtesy of Lauren Bernhardt-Rhone

Calypso & Clovis

Calypso was a Northern Resident female Orca from the A pod off the coast of British Columbia, Canada. In December of 1970, at only six years old, she was captured in Pender Harbor, British Columbia, Canada. After being transported temporarily to Cleethorpes Marineland and Zoo in England while repairs were being made on her tank, she was then moved to Marineland in Antibes, France where she was held for one year. Calypso was the first Orca ever artificially inseminated, however, the procedure was unsuccessful. The sperm used to inseminate Calypso was from an Orca named Cuddles, a captured Southern Resident Orca. At only seven years old, a mere year after being taken from her family in the wild, Calypso died from a lung abscess. She was about 4,400 lbs. and 16.9 ft. long. The Calypso is Greek for "conceal".

Clovis was a two-year-old male Southern Resident Orca captured on August 8th, 1970 from Penn Cove, Washington, USA. He was transported to Marineland Antibes, France where he lived alongside Calypso. Southern Residents and Northern Residents are different populations with completely different dialects, and as such, these two populations would not interact. After Calypso passed away, Clovis was alone in his tank for two and half years. He died in 1973 from myositis. Clovis in French means "Name of a King".

Calypso

Keto

Keto is a male Orca that currently resides at Loro Parque in the Canary Islands. He was born at SeaWorld Orlando and at the age of three he pushed a trainer around the pool with his mouth open. At age 3 ½ he was taken from his mother and shipped to SeaWorld San Diego. In San Diego he swam into a trainer with his mouth open and later the same year he snapped at a trainer. After a year he was shipped to SeaWorld Ohio and in 2001 he was shipped to San Antonio. In 2002 at SeaWorld San Antonio, he swam into a trainer again with his mouth open.

Keto was moved between all four SeaWorld parks before being shipped to the Canary Islands in February 2006 on a breeding loan. On December 24, 2009 Alexis Martinez was performing a stand-on spy hop (an example of this"trick" on bottom right) with Keto, but fell off. Keto was subsequently not bridged (rewarded) for his not so perfect behavior. Alexis attempted a second stand-on spy hop, but again failed resulting in Keto once again not being rewarded. Keto was then ordered over to the side of the pool and when he obeyed, the trainer rewarded him with fish. Alexis then asked Keto for a behavior called a haul out in which Alexis is pushed from the bottom of the pool to the stage. As the two were descending, Alexis decided against the behavior and instead rose to the surface holding Keto's rostrum. Keto was not awarded for the attempted behavior. Keto was called over to the side of the pool, but when he obeyed he was not given a reward. The trainer had asked someone to bring him some fish, but for some reason it was not given to Keto. Alexis started to swim to the side of the pool when Keto went after him. The 6,600 lb. Orca pulled Alexis by his leg to the bottom of the 36-foot pool. By the time trainers were able to get Keto into a separate pool, Alexis had been underwater for almost three minutes. The autopsy report concluded that Alexis sustained collapsed lungs, fractures to the ribs and sternum, a lacerated liver, and bite marks.

Loro Parque
Photo courtesy of Britta Lenzner

Stand-on Spy Hop
Photo by Tiffany Humphrey

Luna

Luna, also known as L98 or Tsu'xiit, was a male Southern Resident Orca born in 1999 off the waters of Washington State. In July 2001 Luna was seen traveling alone in Nootka Sound on the west coast of Vancouver Island, B.C. He was two years old when separated from his pod and researchers were worried he would not survive alone. Despite researchers concerns, Luna was in good shape and was seen fishing for salmon. It was speculated that Luna got separated from his mother and pod and remained in the area awaiting their return. Some thought that he was traveling with his uncle Orcan (L39) and when his uncle died he was left in an unfamiliar area. The Department of Fisheries and Oceans (DFO) monitored Luna to ensure his safety from passing or curious boats which Luna had a tendency to follow and push around with his rostrum.

Around that same time, Springer (A73), a lone Northern Resident young Orca was spotted traveling near Seattle. Springer was eventually taken by boat to Canadian waters where she was reunited with her pod.

In August 2003, Luna was struck by a boat propeller and sustained a six-inch gash on his head. In the summer of 2004, the Canadian and US Governments made arrangements to catch Luna in a sea pen and reunite him with his pod. Plans changed when the Mowachaht/Muchalaht First Nation told the DFO that Luna embodied the spirit of their late chief Ambrose Maquinna, who died three days before Luna showed up in the Sound, and they did not want him captured. The Natives wanted to lead Luna down the west coast of Vancouver in their canoes in order to be reunited with his pod. An agreement was made between the First Nation and DFO to monitor Luna on a permanent basis in the Nootka Sound until a reunion could be attempted.

After Luna disabled boats and gillnets between 2004 and 2005, some called for him to be sent to an aquarium or killed although thousands of tourists traveled to the area just to see the friendly Orca up close. On March 10, 2006 Luna was playing near the 104-foot tugboat General Jackson when he was pulled towards the propeller that was powered by a 1,700 hp engine and killed. Luna lived alone near Vancouver Island for nearly five years.

A12 SATURDAY, JULY 30, 2005 

VANCOUVER PROVINCE, CANWEST NEWS SERVICE, FILE

Luna the killer whale creates a large splash as he leaps behind the canoes leading him to safer waters. The orca is annoying boaters who have suffered boat damage and have been frightened by his antics.

Life of Luna the whale in danger if his playful ways can't be curbed

New approach needed to distract rambunctious, solitary orca

JUDITH LAVOIE
Victoria Times Colonist
VICTORIA

The life of Luna, a solitary whale in Nootka Sound off the west coast of Vancouver Island, is in danger unless someone rapidly distracts him from his boisterous play habits, say two authors who are proposing a new approach to dealing with the five-year-old orca.

Luna is exuberantly playing with small recreational boats. In the last two weeks, several vessels have been damaged and boaters have been alarmed by the whale's antics.

While people are encouraged to stay away from Luna so he does not get habituated to people, two science writers say that hasn't worked and a different approach is called for.

"We think the only way to keep this highly social animal alive is to give him a human family until his whale family comes to get him," said Suzanne Chisholm, who, along with Michael Parfit, has been working in the Nootka Sound area for 18 months.

The 18-page proposal, which is being studied by DFO, calls for the two to put together a scientific team, under a DFO permit, which would provide Luna with the company and entertainment he craves, while keeping him away from risky situations.

The aim is to "prevent dangerous interaction, to realize opportunities for research and to increase the chances that Luna will survive to eventually reunite with his pod," the proposal says.

The team would work in conjunction with the Mowachaht/Muchalaht First Nation — which scuttled last year's attempts to capture Luna and reunite him with his pod — and no extra money would be needed from DFO, Parfit said.

Scientific organizations have already expressed interest in the year-round, long-term program which would allow scientists to study the whale, Parfit said.

It is also hoped that, once Luna develops an affinity for the project boat, his territory could be expanded and he would regularly swim into the open ocean where there is more chance he would connect with pod members.

It is a fallacy to think Luna does not already have ample interaction with people, but no one talks about it because playing with the whale is against the law, Parfit said. "Everyone in the province has touched that whale.

"We want to give him what he wants in a managed controlled way with people who are trained. We want to keep him alive and keep him off fishermen's boats."

There are increasing threats to shoot or harpoon Luna or even feed him fish laced with cyanide, said Parfit and Chisholm.

"Killing him would be tragic and dangerous and solves nothing because it would create dramatic conflict among people. But, we understand the frustration. We think the threat is terribly real," Parfit said.

CanWest News Service

Newspaper Clipping from the
Edmonton Journal
July 30, 2005

Miracle

A two-year-old lone female Orca was spotted on the east coast of Vancouver Island in the summer of 1977. Bill Davis, a fisherman, befriended Miracle and fed her fish out of his hand, something that had never been done before in the wild. Sealand of the Pacific obtained a permit to capture the Southern Resident whale for their aquarium. When Miracle was captured she had propeller wounds, a bullet wound, and several parasites covering her body. After arriving in Victoria, she sank to the bottom of her pool and was presumed dead. Miracle however made several rebounds, hence her name. She remained at Sealand with a male Orca named Haida until 1982. In January 1982, Miracle was found dead between the two containment sections of her pool. Her death was speculated to have been the cause of drowning after being caught in the netting. Captain Paul Watson investigated the death of Miracle at the time and found that there was evidence of a deliberate attempt to cut the net, but cutting was incomplete, which may have been caused by the arrival of a security guard. There was one suspect, but inconclusive evidence. She was in captivity from 1977 to 1982 and died at the age of seven.

Miracle being moved to a sea pen

CHAPTER 3: The Deceased

During the writing of this book, Tilikum, Kasatka, and Kayla passed away.

We removed their pages from the Currently Enslaved Whales and added them to the deceased in this chapter.

Tilikum's story can also be found in Chapter 2: The Famous

Kasatka and Kayla's information can be found after the tombstones in this chapter

Health Hazards for Orcas in Captivity at Sea World

The history of captivity of Orcas has demonstrated that Orca confinement is extremely unhealthy. Here is a list of some of the detrimental impacts on health and the cause of death of many captive Orcas.

1. Tooth Decay: Many of the Orcas in captivity bite on steel gates and the concrete sides of their cells. Fractured teeth lead to exposed pulps, which can cause infections. Holes are drilled (without anesthetics) into the affected teeth and rinsed out three times a day with an iodine/saline solution. Kalina, a 25-year-old female died on October 4th, 2010 of acute bacterial Septicemia. Her dental history before her death included five drilled teeth and four pulled teeth.
2. Pneumonia: Joel Manby made a big deal about Keiko dying of pneumonia insinuating that the cause of Keiko's death was pneumonia that resulted from him being freed to the sea. This despite the fact that Keiko died five years after being released. He conveniently forgot to mention that nine Orcas died of pneumonia at Sea World since 1971. In fact, bacterial pneumonia is the most common cause of death for captive dolphins and Orcas. Captive Orcas suffer from immunosuppression leaving them susceptible to infections including pneumonia – one of the many reasons they are fed large quantities of antibiotics on a daily basis.
3. Kidney failure: Canuck II died of kidney disease at Sea World in 1981 at the age of six, after four years in the tanks. Orky II lost 2 tons of weight before dying at Sea World in 1988. SeaWorld's necropsy report records the cause of death as kidney failure.
4. Infections: Sea World regularly treats their Orcas with antibiotics and there is reason to believe this can lead to drug-resistant infections. In December 2015, Unna died at the age of 19 of Candida, a fungal injection. Sea World attempted to say that Candida was common amongst wild Orcas but this claim has no scientific validity.
5. Mosquito Transmitted Diseases: Orcas in captivity spend far more time floating at the surface than in the wild and trainers have reported large swarms of mosquitoes on their backsides. In 1990, a 25-year-old male Orca named Kanduke died at Sea World Orlando from St. Louis Encephalitis Virus. In 2007, a 14-year-old Orca died of West Nile virus at SeaWorld San Antonio. The other six Orcas in San Antonio also tested positive for West Nile. There has not been a single case of either virus found in wild Orcas.
6. UV Damage – Due to extended periods of logging at the surface, retinal damage can occur from looking up at the sun and Orcas often times get sun burnt, requiring black zinc oxide to be applied to their skin.
7. Collapsed dorsal fins – All of the adult male Orcas in captivity have collapsed dorsal fins as well as most females. This is an extremely rare occurrence in the wild and is usually associated with human interaction (pollution, entanglement). Some speculated reasons for dorsal fin collapse are insufficient support due to logging at the surface, dehydration, and stress.
8. Dehydration – Most of the Orcas in captivity are fed gelatin cubes referred to as JELL-O. The tasteless cubes are given in large quantities in order to supplement the water deficiencies from eating frozen-thawed fish.
9. Psychological disorders – Boredom, stress and unnatural social groups cause Orcas to act out in frustration, whether it be biting walls, pulling paint stripes from the wall or ramming gates. Hugo, a male Orca who resided with Lolita at the Miami Seaquarium, routinely rammed his head into the walls of his pool. This repeated behavior ultimately caused his demise as he rammed his head into the wall on March 4, 1980 and died (see appendix for photo).

Kotar's death is officially listed as acute hemorrhagic pneumonia but what caused this was a metal gate closing on his head and fracturing his skull. Due to numerous deaths, Sea World no longer releases necropsy reports. Now the facility needs only to report the death without an obligation to report the cause. The necropsy report is added to the MMIR (Marine Mammal Inventory Report) but only the National Marine Fisheries Service (NMFS) has access to those details.

Ahab
1959 – 1974
Captured 1968
Died age 15
Unknown causes

Ai
1988 – 1995
Captured 1989
Died age 7
Candidiasis
(fungal infection)

Algonquin
1999 – 2002
Captive Born
Died age 2
Twisted intestine

April
2004 – 2004
Captive Born
Died age 24 days
Malnutrition

Asuka
1990 – 2007
Captured 1997
Died age 17
Unknown causes

Athena
2004 – 2009
Captive Born
Died age 4
Unknown causes

Baby Shamu II
1986 – 1986
Captive Born
Died age 11 days
Heart defect

Belen (Bethlehem)
1987 – 2000
Captured 1988
Died age 13
Unknown causes

Benkei
1969 – 1989
Captured 1979
Died age 20
Acute pneumonia

Benkei II
1979 – 1983
Captured 1980
Died age 4
Malignant lymphoma

Benkei III
1981 – 1983
Captured 1982
Died age 2
(1 year after capture)
Unknown causes

Betty
1974 – 1987
Captured 1978
Died age 13
Pneumonia

Bjossa
1978 – 2001
Captured 1980
Died age 22
Chronic
bronchopneumonia

Bjossa's Calf
1988 – 1988
Captive Born
Died age 21 days
Malnutrition

Bjossa's Calf
1995 – 1995
Captive Born
Died minutes after birth
Ruptured
umbilical cord

Bonnie
1964 – 1968
Captured 1968
Died age 4
(4 months after capture)
Heart failure

Calypso
1959 – 1970
Captured 1969
Died age 11
(1 year after capture)
Lung abscess

Canuck
1970 – 1974
Captured 1972
Died age 4
Candidiasis

Canuck II
1975 – 1981
Captured 1977
Died age 6
Chronic kidney disease

Caren
1976 – 1987
Captured 1979
Died age 11
Agranulocytosis
(low white blood cell count)

Chappy
1969 – 1974
Captured 1970
Died age 5
Periostitis of
lumbar bone

Chi
1966 – 1979
Captured 1979
Died age 13
(2 months after capture)
Unknown causes

Chimo
1968 – 1972
Captured 1970
Died age 4
Pneumonia
(had Chediak-Higashi
syndrome – albinism)

Clovis
1966 – 1973
Captured 1970
Died age 7
Myositis (inflammation
of muscle tissue)

Corky
1963 – 1970
Captured 1968
Died age 7
Mediastinal abscess

Corky II's Calf
1977 -1977
Captive Born
Died age 15 days
Brain damage

Corky II's Calf
1985 – 1985
Captive Born
Died age 29 days
Asphyxiation

Cuddles
1968 – 1974
Captured 1968
Died age 6
Streptococcal
mediastinal abscess

Dzul-Ha
1976 – 1983
Captured 1979
Died age 7
Unknown causes

Finna
1977 – 1997
Captured 1980
Died age 20
Pneumonia

Frankie
1962 – 1974
Captured 1973
Died age 12
(7 months after capture)
Influenza

Freya
1981 – 2015
Captured 1982
Died age 33
Unknown causes

Freyja (Patty)
1980 – 1987
Captured 1984
Died age 7
Acute enteritis
(inflammation
of the intestine)

Goro
1984 – 2005
Captured 1985
Died age 21
Acute pneumonia

Gundrun
1976 – 1996
Captured 1976
Died age 20
Bacteremia associated
with endomyometritis
Died a week after a miscarriage

Haida
1963 – 1982
Captured 1968
Died age 19
Lung infection

HAIDA II
1981 – 2001
CAPTURED 1982
DIED AGE 20
NECROSIS OF CEREBRUM

HAIDA II'S CALF
1994 – 1994
CAPTIVE BORN
DIED AGE 38 DAYS
PNEUMONIA MULTIFOCAL PYOGRANULOMATOUS

HALYN
2005 – 2008
CAPTIVE BORN
DIED AGE 2
ACUTE NECROTIZING ENCEPHALITIS
(INFLAMMATION OF THE BRAIN)

HOI WAI (PEANUTS)
1975 – 1997
CAPTURED 1977
DIED AGE 22
SEVERE INTESTINAL BLOOD LOSS

HUDSON
1998 – 2004
CAPTIVE BORN
DIED AGE 6
MENINGITIS

HUGO
1965 – 1980
CAPTURED 1968
DIED AGE 15
ANEURYSM CEREBRAL ARTERY
(AFTER BASHING HEAD INTO POOL WALL)

HYAK II
1967 – 1991
CAPTURED 1968
DIED AGE 24
PNEUMONIA

JUMBO
1964 – 1974
CAPTURED 1970
DIED AGE 10
LIVER DYSFUNCTION

JUNIOR
1982 – 1994
CAPTURED 1984
DIED AGE 12
BRAIN DAMAGE

KAHANA
1976 – 1991
CAPTURED 1978
DIED AGE 15
SEVERE HEAD TRAUMA
(SLAMMED HEAD INTO WALL)

KALINA
1985 – 2010
CAPTIVE BORN
DIED AGE 25
ACUTE BACTERIAL SEPTICEMIA
(INFECTION OF THE BLOOD)

KANDU
1965 – 1971
CAPTURED 1967
DIED AGE 6
PNEUMONIA,
LIVER NECROSIS

KANDU II
1968 – 1979
CAPTURED 1971
DIED AGE 11
PNEUMONIA

KANDU III
1968 – 1975
CAPTURED 1971
DIED AGE 7
URAEMIA (UREA IN THE BLOOD)
NEPHRITIS
(KIDNEY INFLAMMATION)

KANDU V
1974 – 1989
CAPTURED 1977
DIED AGE 15
MAXILLARY BILATERAL FRACTURE
(RAMMED INTO CORKY)

KANDU VII
1978 – 2005
CAPTURED 1984
DIED AGE 27
CANCER

KANDUKE (KANDU IV)
1965 – 1990
CAPTURED 1975
DIED AGE 25
VIRAL LEPTOMENINGITIS

KANDY
1959 – 1973
CAPTURED 1973
DIED AGE 14
(3 MONTHS AFTER CAPTURE)
ACUTE PNEUMONIA

KANUCK
1994 – 1998
CAPTIVE BORN
DIED AGE 4
TRAUMATIC SHOCK

KASATKA
1976 – 2017
CAPTURED 1978
DIED AGE 41
LUNG DISEASE

KATERINA
1988 – 1999
CAPTIVE BORN
DIED AGE 10
BACTERIAL PNEUMONIA

KATY
1966 – 1967
CAPTURED 1967
DIED AGE 1
(3 MONTHS AFTER CAPTURE)
UNKNOWN CAUSES

KAYLA
1988-2019
CAPTIVE BORN
DIED AT AGE 31
LUNG DISEASE

KENAU
1974 -1991
CAPTURED 1976
DIED AGE 17
BACTERIAL PNEUMONIA

KENNY
1965 – 1972
CAPTURED 1969
DIED AGE 7
PNEUMONIA

KIANU
1952 – 1980
CAPTURED 1968
DIED AGE 28
GASTROINTESTINAL DISEASE

KILROY
1965 – 1978
CAPTURED 1967
DIED AGE 13
GANGRENOUS PNEUMONIA

KIM
1968 – 1982
CAPTURED 1976
DIED AGE 14
LUNG ABSCESS

KIM II
1978 – 2005
CAPTURED 1982
DIED AGE 27
PNEUMONIA

KING
1977 – 1983
CAPTURED 1979
DIED AGE 6
ACUTE PNEUMONIA

KISKA'S CALF
1992 – 1992
CAPTIVE BORN
DIED AGE 2 MONTHS
DROWNING

KIVA
1982 – 1982
CAPTIVE BORN
DIED AGE 1.5 MONTHS
RESPIRATORY FAILURE

KONA
1965 – 1977
CAPTURED 1971
DIED AGE 12
SEPTICEMIA

KONA II
1975 – 1987
CAPTURED 1977
DIED AGE 12
PULMONARY ABSCESSION

KOTAR
1976 – 1995
CAPTURED 1978
DIED AGE 19
ACUTE HEMORRHAGIC PNEUMONIA (METAL GATE FELL AND CRUSHED HEAD)

KU
1992 – 2008
CAPTURED 1997
DIED AGE 16
HEART FAILURE

Kyara
2017 – 2017
Captive Born
Died age 3 months
pneumonia

Kyosha
1991 – 1992
Captive Born
Died age 3 months
Brain infection

Kyu
1987 – 2004
Captured 1997
Died age 17
Bacterial pneumonia

Lil Nooka
1968 – 1971
Captured 1970
Died age 3
(7 months after capture)
Asphyxiation

Lupa
1956 – 1968
Captured 1968
Died age 12
(7 months after capture)
Pneumonia

Maggie
1983 – 1997
Captured 1987
Died age 14
Birth complications

Maggie's Calf
1995 – 1995
Captive Born
Died age 1 day
Unknown causes

Magnus
1974 – 1977
Captured 1977
Died age 3
(2 months after capture)
Agranulocytic anaemia

Malik
1996 – 2000
Captive Born
Died age 3
Immune system deficiency

Mamuk
1964 – 1974
Captured 1968
Died age 10
Acute streptococcal septicemia

Milagro
1981 – 1991
Captured 1985
Died age 10
Unknown causes

Miracle
1975 – 1982
Captured 1977
Died age 7
Drowning

Moby Doll
1957 – 1964
Captured 1964
Died age 7
(2.5 months after capture)
Drowning

Nami
1983 – 2011
Captured 1985
Died age 28
Pulmonary zygomycosis
(fungal infection)

Namu
1955 – 1966
Captured 1965
Died age 11
(1 year after capture)
Drowning

Nandu
1980 – 1988
Captured 1983
Died age 8
Adrenal gland tumor

Natsidalia
1953 – 1968
Captured 1968
Died age 15
(7 months after capture)
Heart failure

Nemo
1978 – 1986
Captured 1981
Died age 8
Thrombocytosis
(excessive platelets in blood)

Neocia
1992 – 2004
Captive Born
Died age 11
Internal infection

Nepo
1966 – 1980
Captured 1969
Died age 14
Acute bronchopneumonia

Neptune
1977 – 1983
Captured 1981
Died age 6
(1.7 year after capture)
Appendicitis

No Name
Age unknown
Captured 1978
Died in 1979
(3 months in captivity)
Heart attack

No Name
Age unknown
Captured 1978
Died in 1979
(3 months in captivity)
Pneumonia

No Name
1964 – 1979
Captured 1979
Died age 15
(1 month after capture)
Birth complications

No Name
Age unknown
Captured 1979
Died in 1979
(2 months in captivity)
Nutritional disorder

No Name
1977 – 1980
Captured 1979
Died age 3
(2 months after capture)
Acute enterotoxemia
(blood poisoning)

No Name
1979 – 1981
Captured 1981
Died age 2
(1 month after capture)
Traumatic shock, ruptured kidney

No Name
1969 – 1982
Captured 1982
Died age 13
(4 months after capture)
Pneumonia

No Name
1980 – 1983
Captured 1982
Died age 3
(8 months after capture)
Haemophilia

No Name
1982 – 1985
Captured 1984
Died age 3
(2 months after capture)
Neck injury

No Name
Age unknown
Captured 1986
Died in 1986
(2 months after capture)
Unknown causes

No Name
1993 – 1997
Captured 1997
Died age 4
(4 months after capture)
Systemic viral infection (herpes)

No Name
1977 – 1997
Captured 1997
Died age 20
(4 months after capture)
Bacterial pneumonia

No Name
1997 – 2003
Captured 2003
Died age 6
(1 month after capture)
Unknown causes

No Name
2002 – 2006
Captured 2006
Died age 4
(3 days after capture)
Unknown causes

No Name
Age unknown
Captured 1969
Date of death unknown
Unknown causes

No Name
Age unknown
Captured 1970
Date of death unknown
Unknown causes
Seattle Marine
Aquarium

No Name
Age unknown
Captured 1971
Date of death unknown
Unknown causes
Seattle Marine
Aquarium

No Name
Age unknown
Captured 1971
Date of death unknown
Unknown causes
Seattle Marine
Aquarium

No Name
Age unknown
Captured 1981
Date of death unknown
Unknown causes
Marineland
of Canada

No Name
Age unknown
Captured 1992
Died age 1992
Unknown causes
Mundo Marino
Argentina

Nootka
1962 – 1990
Captured 1970
Died age 28
Pyogranulomatous

Nootka II
1944 – 1974
Captured 1973
Died age 30
(9 months after capture)
Ruptured aorta

Nootka III
1972 – 1976
Captured 1975
Died age 4
(8.5 months after capture)
Perforated pyloric ulcer

Nootka IV
1980 – 1994
Captured 1982
Died age 14
Septicemia
Died in pre-operation,
1 month after stillbirth

Nootka IV's Calf
1992 – 1992
Captive born
Died age 1 month
Infection; high white
blood cell count

Nootka V
1976 – 2008
Captured 1981
Died age 32
Unknown causes

Nootka V's Calf
1998 – 1998
Captive born
Died age 10 days
Unknown causes

Nova
1996 – 2001
Captive born
Died age 4
Starvation

Nyar
1993 – 1996
Captive born
Died age 2
Suppurative encephalitis
had mental problems

Orky
1960 – 1969
Captured 1967
Died age 9
(1.11 years after capture)
Pneumonia

Orky II
1958 – 1988
Captured 1968
Died age 30
Acute bronchopneumonia
nephropathy

Oscar
1985 – 2012
Captured 1987
Died age 27
Unknown causes

Pascuala
2007 – 2007
Rescued 2007
Died age 2 months
Malnutrition

Patches
1963 – 1971
Captured 1969
Died age 8
(1.8 years after capture)
Mediastinal abscess

Prince
1982 – 1991
Captured 1987
Died age 9
Pseudomonas

Ramu
1964 – 1982
Captured 1967
Died age 18
Cause listed as old age

Ramu II
1955 – 1970
Captured 1969
Died age 15
(1.2 years after capture)
Unknown causes

Ramu IV
1968 – 1971
Captured 1970
Died age 3
(1 year after capture)
Unknown causes

Ran
1988 – 2004
Captured 1989
Died age 16
Unknown causes
Birthed a premature calf
3 days before death

Ran's Calf
2004 – 2004
Captive born
Died age 2 days
Broken skull

Ruka
1979 – 2000
Captured 1981
Died age 21
Traumatic shock

Sacchi
1971 – 1984
Captured 1982
Died age 13
(2.2 years after capture)
Pneumonia

Sacchi's Calf
1982 – 1982
Captive born
Died age 10 days
Brain abscess

Samoa
1978 – 1992
Captured 1983
Died age 14
Mycotic
meningoencephalitis

Sandy
1966 – 1977
Rescued 1973
Died age 11
Cerebral hemorrhage

Sarah
2003 – 2006
Captured 2003
Died age 2
Unknown causes

Scarred Jaw Cow
1950 – 1970
Captured 1970
Died age 20
(2.5 months after capture)
Malnutrition

Shachi
1976 – 1988
Captured 1986
Died age 12
(2 years after capture)
Pneumonia

Shamu
1962 – 1971
Captured 1965
Died age 9
Septicemia

Sharkan
1986 – 2009
Captured 1989
Died age 23
Bacillus pyocyanique

Shawn
1977 – 1979
Captured 1978
Died age 2
(1.8 years after capture)
Pneumonia

Skana
1961 – 1980
Captured 1967
Died age 19
Mycotic (fungal) infection

Splash
1989 – 2005
Captive born
Died age 15
Acute perforating gastric ulceration

Spooky
1978 – 1978
Captive Born
Died age 10 days
Colitis

Sumar
1998 – 2010
Captive Born
Died age 12
Gastric torsion

Surfer Girl
1978 – 1979
Rescued 1979
Died age 1
(7 days after rescue)
Kidney failure, perforated gastric ulcer

Tai
1969 – 1982
Captured 1979
Died age 13
Unknown causes

Taiji
Age unknown
Captured 1978
Died in 1978
(5 days after capture)
Died of harpoon wound
Japan

Taima
1989 – 2010
Captive born
Died age 20
Peracute uterine prolapse during labor

Taku
1993 – 2007
Captive born
Died age 14
Multifocal interstitial pneumonia

Tanouk
1986 – 2000
Captured 1989
Died age 14
Unknown causes

Tilikum
1981 – 2017
Captured 1983
Died age 36
Lung infection

Tula
1965 – 1968
Captured 1968
Died age 3
(3 months after capture)
External fungus

Unna
1996 – 2015
Captive born
Died age 18
Candida

Valentin
1996 – 2015
Captive born
Died age 9
Twisted intestines

Victoria
2012 – 2013
Captive born
Died age 10 months
Intestinal complications

Vigga
1977 – 2000
Captured 1980
Died age 23
Heart failure

Wanda
1951 –1961
Captured 1961
Died age 10
(2 days after capture)
Gastroenteritis
(rammed into pool)

Whale
1969 – 1971
Captured 1970
Died age 2
(1.2 years after capture)
Heart failure

Winnie
1975 – 2002
Captured 1977
Died age 27
GI tract obstruction

Winston
1963 – 1986
Captured 1970
Died age 23
Chronic cardiovascular failure

Yaka
1965 – 1997
Captured 1969
Died age 32
Upper respiratory infection

Zero
Age unknown
Captured 1972
Died in 1972
(2 weeks after capture)
Harpoon wound

Kasatka

1976 est	October 1978	1978	1982	1987	1988	1990	2017
Born	Captured in Iceland	Sent to San Diego	Sent to Ohio	Sent to Orlando	Sent to San Antonio	Sent to San Diego	Passed Away

Species: Orcinus orca
Breed: 100% Icelandic
Meaning of name: Russian for "killer whale"
Captivity History: Captured in October 1978 in the waters off Iceland around 1-2 years old
Offspring: Takara (1991), Nakai (2001), Kalia (2004), Makani (2013)
Sex: Female
Weight: 4,860 lbs.
Length: 17.3 ft.

Kasatka has been moved around between all four SeaWorld parks. She was the first Orca to be successfully artificially inseminated in 2000 by Tilikum. She became the dominant female at San Diego in 1989 after Kandu died. No one was allowed to get into the water with Kasatka after a 2006 incident. During the writing of this book, Kasatka passed away. Kasatka was euthanized on August 16, 2017 after suffering from lung disease.

Incidents:
1989 - mouthed the leg of a trainer on two occasions
1990 - mouthed the thigh of a trainer
1991 - grabbed the foot of a trainer
1992 - she mouthed the foot a trainer
1993 - mouthed the feet and legs of a trainer and later, grabbed a trainer and dunked him underwater
1999 - SeaWorld San Diego, she lifted Ken Peters out of the water
2004 - mouthed the fins of a trainer in SCUBA gear
2006 - dragged Ken Peters down to the bottom of the pool three times
2008 – came out of the water at trainers three times

SeaWorld San Diego 2007
Photo courtesy of Heather Jordan

Kayla

November 26, 1988	1991	1999	November 2006	January 28, 2019
Born at SW San Antonio	Sent to SW Ohio	Sent to SW San Antonio	Sent to SW Orlando	Passed Away

Species: Orcinus orca
Breed: 50% Icelandic, 50% Northern Resident
Meaning of name: Arabic for "wise child" and English for "pure"
Captivity history: Born at SeaWorld San Antonio
Mother: Kenau
Father: Orky II
Offspring: Halyn (2005), Miscarriage (2007)
Sex: Female
Weight: 5,600 lbs.
Length: 19 ft.

Kayla was the first Orca born at SeaWorld San Antonio. She was separated from her mother and moved to SeaWorld Ohio at the young age of 2. In 1992 she pushed a trainer. In 1996, a guest tried to touch Kayla and she thrashed her head side to side with her mouth open. In 1999, Kayla was sent back to SeaWorld San Antonio. In 2003, she came at a trainer with her mouth open and motioned towards a trainer's hand with mouth open. In 2004, she lunged at a trainer. In 2005, she gave birth to a female calf named Halyn but rejected her. In October 2006, she lunged at trainer with mouth open throwing him several feet. A month later she lunged at a trainer knocking a bucket off of a wall. A pregnant Kayla was shipped to SeaWorld Orlando in November 2006 in order to teach her how to care for calves. In 2007 Kayla suffered a miscarriage. Kayla died in 2019 from lung disease.

Kayla on left
Photo courtesy of Lauren Bernhardt-Rhone

CHAPTER 4: Currently Enslaved Whales

On the following pages, you will find a brief description of each Orca in captivity. As a result of the highly publicized case in 2011, Secretary of Labor v. SeaWorld of Florida, LLC, SeaWorld Orca profiles were made available to the public. Not all incidents were recorded, but the profiles give you an indication as to the amount of frustration the animals endure. Dangers occur in animal training when control is broken between animal and trainer. The profiles were written to learn certain precursors from individual animals in order to anticipate when an aggressive act might occur. Precursors are extremely important, but not all animals give them, making it impossible to know when an animal might break from control. There are many incidents listed in this chapter such as "mouthing" or "lunging with mouth open" which are clear signs that the animal has broken from control and could potentially injure someone. "Mouthing" at a bootie might not sound dangerous, however, these are 5,000 to 12,000 pound carnivores capable of causing death with one single blow. A surfer in 1972 reported an Orca grabbed his leg, but released him resulting in one hundred stitches. No human deaths by Orcas have been recorded in the wild. Even during the large violent captures off the coast of Washington State and British Columbia, there were no injuries inflicted to any humans by the whales. Even when babies were ripped away from mothers, the whales still caused no injuries or death to one single person.

Four humans have been killed by Orcas and all four took place at marine parks;
Keltie Byrne –1991 – SeaLand of the Pacific – Orca, Tilikum
Daniel Dukes – 1999 – SeaWorld Orlando – Orca, Tilikum
Alexis Martinez – 2009 – Loro Parque – Orca, Keto
Dawn Brancheau – 2010 – SeaWorld Orlando – Orca, Tilikum

Many Orcas have been shuffled between parks so their locations are at times fluid. In the midst of writing this book, several whales have passed away, were born, and some moved locations. We cannot guarantee that all of the data in this book will be up to date by the time it goes to print, however, we did our best to update the status of every whale while in the process of compiling our data.

Notes:
*ML refers to Marineland
*SW refers to SeaWorld

Moskvarium
Moscow, Russia
Naja, Narnia, Nord
3
Marineland
Antibes, France
Inouk, Keijo,
Moana, Wikie
4
SeaWorld
San Diego, California, USA
Amaya, Corky II, Ikaika,
Kalia, Keet, Makani,
Nakai, Orkid,
Shouka, Ulises,
10
MarineLand
Niagara Falls,
Ontario, Canada
Kiska
1
Miami
SeaAquarium
Miami, Florida, USA
Lolita
1
SeaWorld
San Antonio, Texas, USA
Kamea, Kyuquot,
Sakari, Takara, Tuar
5
SeaWorld
Orlando, Florida, USA
Katina, Makaio, Malia,
Nalani, Trua
5
Loro Parque
Canary Islands, Spain
Adan, Keto, Kohana,
Morgan, Skyla,
Tekoa, Ula
7
Mundo Marino
Argentina
South America
Kshamenk
1

Seaside Dolphinarium
Nakhodka, Russia
Malvina
1
Kamogawa SeaWorld
Chiba, Japan
Lara, Lovey, Luna, Ran II
4
Port of Nagoya
Nagoya, Japan
Earth, Stella, Rin
3
Shanghai Haichang Ocean Park
Shanghai, China
Dora, Wow, 2 Unnamed
4
Wuxi Changqiao Ocean Kingdom
Wuxi, China
Unnamed, Unnamed
2
Chimelong Ocean Kingdom
Hengqin, Zhuhai, China
Grace, Nukka, Orpheus, Tyson, 5 Unnamed
9

SEAWORLD ORLANDO, FLORIDA, USA

1991 – Photo courtesy of Olaf Schmidt

Founded: 1973

Held Orcas Since: 1975

Location: Orlando, Florida, USA

Dimensions:

Show Pool – 36 ft deep x 190 ft long x 90 ft wide

Back Pool – 70 ft long x 25 ft deep. Back Pool – 70 ft long x 25 ft deep

Shading Tank – 100 ft long x 20 ft deep

Medical Pool – 20 ft long

Underwater Viewing Tank – 36 ft deep x 220 ft long x 70 ft wide

Water: 6M gallons

Orcas: 5 (Katina, Makaio, Malia, Nalani, Trua)

Katina

1975 est	October 1978	October 1978	1978 - 1979	June 1979 – 1984	1984
Born	Captured	Sent to Hafnarfjordur	Sent to ML Ontario	Moved between SW San Diego and Ohio	Sent to SW Orlando

Species: Orcinus orca
Breed: 100% Icelandic
Meaning of name: Greek for “pure”
Captivity history:
Captured at age 3 near Skardsfjara, Iceland
Offspring: Kalina (1985), Katerina (1988), Taku (1993), Unna (1996), Ikaika (2002), Nalani (2006), Makaio (2010)
Sex: Female
Weight: 5,400 lbs.
Length: 18 ft.

Katina was the first mother to successfully give birth in captivity. She is currently the dominant female at SeaWorld Orlando.

Katina mated with her son Taku and had Nalani in 2006. After the birth, Katina resisted accepting Nalani and would often displace her. Of her seven offspring, five are dead. Her daughter Katerina was taken away at age 2 and sent to SeaWorld Ohio and then SeaWorld San Antonio where she passed away in 1999. Taku passed away in 2006. Ikaika passed away in 2006. Kalina died in 2010. Unna was taken away from Katina at age 6 and sent to SeaWorld San Antonio where she later passed away in 2015.

Katina on right
Photo courtesy of Lauren Bernhardt-Rhone

Incidents:
1989 - mouthed the waist of a trainer
1992 - bumped the hip of a trainer
1993 - bumped the body of a trainer
1994 - bumped the hand of a trainer
1995 - she pushed a trainer

Makaio

October 9, 2010
Born at SeaWorld Orlando

Species: Orcinus orca
Breed: 100% Icelandic
Meaning of name: Hawaiian for "gift of god"
Captivity history: Born at SeaWorld Orlando
Mother: Katina
Father: Tilikum
Full Siblings: Taku, Unna, Ikaika
Offspring: None
Sex: Male
Weight: 2,800 lbs.
Length: 13 ft.

Photo courtesy of Samantha Cornwall
(Instagram @samcorn.swo)

Makaio is Katina's seventh calf. Katina's first calf Kalina passed away on October 4, 2010 only five days before Makaio was born- Kalina was the first calf successfully born in captivity.

In December of 2014, Makaio was almost hit by a closing gate while he was heading to a back pool to be with his mother Katina.

Malia

March 12, 2007
Born at SeaWorld Orlando

Species: Orcinus orca
Breed: 75% Icelandic, 25% Bigg's Transient
Meaning of name: Hawaiian for "calm and peaceful"
Captivity history: Born at SeaWorld Orlando
Mother: Taima
Father: Tilikum
Full Siblings: Sumar, Tekoa
Offspring: None
Sex: Female
Weight: 3,340 lbs.
Length: 15.5 ft.

Kayla & Malia
Photo courtesy of Samantha Cornwall
(Instagram @samcorn.swo)

Malia was born at SeaWorld Orlando. She is Taima's third calf with Tilikum.

Taima has shown aggression towards all of her calves, including Malia.

Malia has had several abnormal behaviors ranging from listing at the surface to no-movement seizure like states. Malia's mother Taima passed away in 2010 of peracute uterine pneumonia when Malia was only 3 years old.

Nalani

September 18, 2006
Born at SeaWorld Orlando

Species: Orcinus orca
Breed: 100% Icelandic
Meaning of name: Hawaiian for "of the heavens"
Captivity history: Born at SeaWorld Orlando
Mother: Katina
Father: Taku
Offspring: None
Sex: Female
Weight: 3,800 lbs.
Length: 16 ft.

Nalani is the first surviving inbred Orca to be born in captivity. Her mother is Katina and her father is Taku. Katina is Taku's mother.

For the first two months of Nalani's life, her mother Katina would often displace her, but Nalani was able to nurse and develop.

(Kohana mated with her uncle Keto and displaced Adan, which was also an inbred calf)

Photo courtesy of Samantha Cornwall (Instagram @samcorn.swo)

Trua

November 23, 2005
Born at SeaWorld Orlando

Species: Orcinus orca
Breed: 100% Icelandic
Meaning of name: Icelandic for "believe"
Captivity history: Born at SeaWorld Orlando
Mother: Takara
Father: Taku
Offspring: None
Sex: Male
Weight: 5,500 lbs.
Length: 18 ft.

Photo courtesy of Samantha Cornwall (Instagram @samcorn.swo)

Trua was born at SeaWorld Orlando in 2005. His mother Takara was moved to SeaWorld San Antonio in 2009 when Trua was only 4 years old.

In 2009, Trua spent months focused on the caulking in one of the pools, resulting in SeaWorld having to remove the entire caulking in that pool.

In captivity, Orcas will focus on things in order to overcome boredom, whether it be regurgitating fish in order to bait birds, peeling the paint off of walls, or biting gate railings.

SEAWORLD SAN ANTONIO, TEXAS, USA

Photo courtesy of PETA

Founded: 1988

Held Orcas Since: 1988

Location: San Antonio, Texas, USA

Dimensions: Show Pool – 40 ft deep x 220 ft long x 150 ft wide; 2M gallons water

Side Pool – 25 ft deep x 115 ft long x 69 ft wide; 998k gallons water

Side Pool – 25 ft deep x 115 ft long x 69 ft wide; 998k gallons water

Medical Pool – 10 ft deep x 26 ft long x 42 ft wide; 60k gallons water

Orcas: 5 (Kamea, Kyuquot, Sakari, Takara, Tuar)

Kamea

December 6, 2013
Born at SeaWorld San Antonio

Species: Orcinus orca
Breed: 50% Icelandic, 50% Argentinian Transient
Meaning of name: Hawaiian for “precious one”
Captivity history: Born at SeaWorld San Antonio
Mother: Takara
Father: Kshamenk
Offspring: None
Sex: Female
Weight: 2,000 lbs.
Length: 12 ft.

Kamea was conceived via artificial insemination to mother Takara by father Kshamenk.

She has never met her father who lives at Mundo Marino in Argentina.

She has no full siblings but she does have four half siblings – Kohana, Trua, Sakari, and Makani. The only half sibling living with her in San Antonio is Sakari.

Kamea with mother Takara
SeaWorld San Antonio
Photo courtesy of PETA

Kyuquot

December 24, 1991
Born at Sealand of the Pacific

January 8, 1993
Sent to SeaWorld San Antonio

Species: Orcinus orca
Breed: 100% Icelandic
Meaning of name: Nootka for "land of many winds"
Captivity history: Born at Sealand of the Pacific
Mother: Haida II
Father: Tilikum
Offspring: Kyara
Sex: Male
Weight: 9,300 lbs.
Length: 22 ft.

Kyuquot, often called Ky, was born at Sealand of the Pacific in 1991. Before Ky was born, Keltie Byrne was killed at the park after Tilikum dragged her into the pool. Sealand of the Pacific shut down and Ky along with his mother Haida II were sent to SeaWorld San Antonio. Ky's mother Haida II died in 2001. In 2016, after several attempts to obtain semen from Ky, they were able to artificially inseminate Takara with his sperm. Ky is the largest Orca at SeaWorld San Antonio as of 2020.

Incidents:
2003 - refused to let a trainer out of the pool
2004 - refused to let trainer Steve Aibel out of the pool, instead pushing him under the water and jumping on him
* These incidents came after the passing of his mother

SeaWorld San Antonio
Photo courtesy of PETA

Sakari

January 7, 2010
Born at SeaWorld San Antonio

Species: Orcinus orca
Breed: 100% Icelandic
Meaning of name: Indian for "sweet"
Captivity history: Born at SeaWorld San Antonio
Mother: Takara
Father: Tilikum
Full Siblings: Kohana
Offspring: None
Sex: Female
Weight: 3,100 lbs.
Length: 14 ft.

Sakari is one of the more dominant Orcas at SeaWorld San Antonio, however, the matriarch of the park is her mother Takara.

John Hargrove stated in an interview regarding Sakari, "She would go down and hit her head on the bottom of the pool, over and over to the point where her jaw would be bloody and bruised...the damage was so bad that Sakari stopped eating for a few days because it was painful for her to open her jaw."

Photo courtesy of PETA

Takara

July 9, 1991
Born at SeaWorld San Diego

2004
Sent to SeaWorld Orlando

February 5, 2009
Sent to SeaWorld San Antonio

Species: Orcinus orca
Breed: 100% Icelandic
Meaning of name: Japanese for "treasure"
Captivity history: Born at SeaWorld San Diego
Mother: Kasatka
Father: Kotar
Offspring: Kohana (2002), Trua (2005), Sakari (2010), Kamea (2013), Kyara (2017)
Sex: Female
Weight: 4,700 lbs.
Length: 17.3 ft.

Takara was born to the matriarch of the Orcas at SeaWorld San Diego, Kasatka. In 1995, she swam over a trainer and in 1999 she came at a trainer aggressively.

Takara was artificially inseminated in 2000 with Tilikum's sperm at age 9. She was the second Orca to ever be successfully artificially inseminated.

In 2004, Takara was moved to SeaWorld Orlando. After Takara was relocated, her mother Kasatka was sending out long-range vocals from her pool, presumably trying to communicate with her. Takara's daughter Kohana was sent to Orlando with her, but they took Kohana away in 2006 and sent her to Loro Parque in Spain. In October 2009, Takara's head slammed into John Hargrove's side breaking his ribs. She is the current dominant whale at SeaWorld San Antonio. Takara's 5th calf, Kyara, was born on April 19, 2017. Takara had conceived Kyara before SeaWorld announced the end of their breeding program. Kyara's father was Kyuquot. Kyara passed away on July 24, 2017 at only 3 months old from an unknown infection.

Takara with daughter Kamea
SeaWorld San Antonio
Photo courtesy of PETA

Tuar

June 22, 1999
Born at SeaWorld Orlando

April 2004
Sent to SeaWorld San Antonio

Species: Orcinus orca
Breed: 75% Icelandic, 25% Southern Resident
Meaning of name: Inukitut for "unique"
Captivity history: Born at SeaWorld Orlando
Mother: Kalina
Father: Tilikum
Full Siblings: Skyla
Offspring: None
Sex: Male
Weight: 7,000 lbs.
Length: 19 ft.

Photo courtesy of Sara Farrell

Tuar was born at SeaWorld Orlando in 1999. In Florida while a trainer was taking something out of Tuar's mouth, he clamped down on the trainer's hand several times.

At the age of 4, he was taken from his mother Kalina and shipped to SeaWorld San Antonio. Tuar has opened his mouth to trainers in Texas and in April 2007, he closed his mouth on a trainer's leg.

Tuar has on several occasions picked paint from the bottom of the pool floor, a sign of boredom.

SEAWORLD SAN DIEGO, CALIFORNIA USA

Photo courtesy of Heather Jordan

Founded: 1964

Held Orcas Since: 1965

Location: San Diego, California, USA

Dimensions:

Show Pool – 36 ft deep x 180 ft long x 90 ft wide; 2.4M gallons water

Side Pool – 15 ft deep x 150 ft long x 80 ft wide; 1M gallons water

Side Pool – 15 ft deep x 150 ft long x 80 ft wide; 1M gallons water

Underwater Viewing Pool – 30 ft deep

Medical Pool – 8 ft deep; 67,600 gallons water

Orcas: 10 (Amaya, Corky II, Ikaika, Kalia, Keet, Makani, Nakai, Orkid, Shouka, Ulises)

Amaya

December 2, 2014
Born at SeaWorld San Diego

Species: Orcinus orca

Breed: 93.75% Icelandic; 6.25 % Southern Resident

Meaning of name: Arabic for "night rain"

Captivity history: Born at SeaWorld San Diego

Mother: Kalia

Father: Ulises

Full Siblings: None

Offspring: None

Sex: Female

Weight: 1,550 lbs.

Length: 11 ft.

Amaya alongside mother Kalia at SeaWorld San Diego
August 5, 2015
Photo courtesy of Anonymous

Amaya was born during a rainstorm, hence her name. Her mother Kalia was nine years old when Amaya was conceived.

Corky II

1966 est	December 11, 1969	1969	1987
Born	Captured in Pender Harbor, BC	Sent to Marineland of Pacific	Sent to SeaWorld San Diego

Species: Orcinus orca
Breed: Northern Resident
Meaning of name: Irish for "hill hollow"
Captivity History: Captured at around age 4 from A5 pod in Pender Harbor, BC
Mother: Stripe (died in the wild in 2000)
Full Siblings: A21, A29, Okisollo, Ripple, Fife
Offspring:
Calf (1977) first Orca ever born in captivity but died after 16 days, Spooky (1978), Stillbirth (1980), Kive (1982), Calf (1985), Miscarriage (1986), Miscarriage (1987)
Sex: Female
Weight: 8,335 lbs.
Length: 20 ft.

SeaWorld San Diego April 12, 2016
Photo courtesy of Anonymous
(notice missing/filed teeth)

Corky II has been in captivity longer than any other Orca. She is about the same age as Lolita, both with estimated birth years of 1966. She has had seven offspring with Orky II, none of which lived past 46 days.
Corky II is the largest female Orca in captivity. On August 21, 1989 Kandu V collided with Corky II, which caused Kandu V to fracture her upper jaw and bleed to death.

Corky II became a surrogate mother to Kandu V's orphaned calf, Orkid after this incident. In 1990, Corky II pushed the mid-section of her trainer and again pushed a trainer in 1994, however, she is known to be a very sweet and gentle Orca.

The author was a kid when she joined The Orca Club and Free Corky Campaign. She wrote a letter to SeaWorld asking them to free Corky. John B. Roberts, Chairman of the Board and President of Busch Entertainment Corporation responded to her letter and included two tickets to the park in his envelope. The author wrote him back and included the ripped up tickets in her envelope.

Busch Entertainment Corporation
ONE OF THE ANHEUSER-BUSCH COMPANIES

John B. Roberts
Chairman of the Board
and President

November 12, 1993

Ms. Tiffany Mayne
13 Midw[redacted]
[redacted]7724

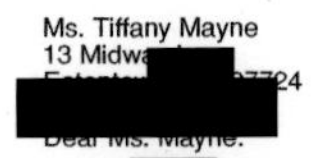

Dear Ms. Mayne:

Thank you for your recent note to August Busch concerning Corky. As President of Busch Entertainment Corporation, I am very encouraged that you care enough about the well-being of animals to take the time to express your opinions about the care of Corky. As a person concerned about animals, I am sure you are eager to hear the facts about this situation so that you can form the best opinion about Corky's well-being. It is for this reason I would like to correct the false and misleading statements made about her recently.

First, I want to assure you that no one cares more about the health and well-being of Corky than Sea World, especially the veterinarians and trainers who have cared for Corky at our park since 1987. In fact, some of those who work with Corky have done so for more than 20 years. As with all of our animals, she receives 24-hour care, and stimulation through relationships with other killer whales and with her trainers. She is fed restaurant-quality fish and receives routine medical examinations to ensure her continued well-being. If the time comes when Corky needs additional medical attention, there is no better place for her to be than Sea World.

If you were to visit Corky at Sea World, you would see firsthand the genuine care and commitment Corky receives. For her trainers, caring for Corky is not a job, it is a part of life. Corky has a strong bond with her human trainers and others who care for her. In addition, Corky is an important part of a group of five killer whales at the park, including two young whales born in the park. It is for one reason only that Sea World will not agree to the proposal to release Corky -- Corky would die. We will not sacrifice her life for a risky "experiment."

To help you better understand our position, I would like to provide some additional facts:

- Corky has been living in the care of humans for almost 24 years, and the most recent scientific studies suggest she is in the later years of her life. Science shows killer whales live to be 25-35 years of age whether they live in the wild or are cared for by humans. Corky is nearly 30 years old, and while her routine medical exams show she's in good health, she is an older animal. Corky's ability to fend for herself in a competitive and uncontrolled world with pollution, parasites, disease and the need to hunt for food is questionable.

Busch Entertainment Corporation
One Busch Place
St. Louis, MO 63118-1852

Ms. Tiffany Mayne
November 12, 1993
Page [redacted]

- Sea World is not alone in its belief that releasing an animal that has lived in the care of human beings for an extended period is inappropriate and unethical. Within the past year, groups of independent marine mammal experts and government panels from Spain and Canada have all reached similar conclusions concerning the inappropriateness of release of animals from zoological settings.

Before concluding, I would like to address one last point. The people at our Sea World parks care for animals because they truly want to make a difference in their well-being and the well-being of future generations of animals. Yes, Sea World is a successful park, but that is why we are able to commit the significant resources necessary to provide our animals with the best in animal care and nutrition, to rescue and rehabilitate stranded animals in need, to conduct research in our parks and in the wild that can be used to help animals today and into the future as well as to educate millions of people about marine life to help preserve our environment for future generations. In just the last two years, Sea World has rescued, rehabilitated and returned to the wild more marine mammals than collected by Sea World during our 28-year history.

I hope you will reconsider your position after reviewing these facts. Having Corky and her fellow killer whales at Sea World has created a respect, love and understanding for these majestic animals that is not possible from reading about them in books or watching film of them on television. Years ago, killer whales were killed for recreational and commercial purposes. Today, that is no longer the case. We believe that high-quality animal programs like Sea World's, which increase the respect for these animals, helped to turn the tide. We are committed to continuing to help people of all ages understand the delicate balance of nature necessary for the survival of the planet and its inhabitants.

Again, thank you for your concern for the welfare of animals. I am sorry to read of your decision concerning our products but hope that after reading this you will reconsider. Enclosed is a certificate good for half off the cost of admission to any of our Sea World parks. I hope you will take advantage of the opportunity to visit us and see our quality care and commitment to animals firsthand.

Sincerely,

John B. Roberts

cc: August A. Busch III

Dear Mr. John B. Roberts,

Thanks for the ticket but personally I don't like watching animals being mistreated.

I'd also like to thank you for writing back. Also for sharing your opinion with me. Although your letter did'nt change my opinion one bit, thanks anyway. I firmly believe that what you're doing is wrong. NOTHING will every change my mind.

You had NO RIGHT to steal Corky from her family. If Corky is going to die soon I think he would want to die with his family. Not with a bunch of strangers. If I were Corky I would want to see my family. If Corky could just see them and swim with them I'm sure that would make her happy. LET HER GO. SHE WANTS TO SEE HER FAMILY!!!!!!!!!!!!!!!!What you're doing is wrong. Do you acuatlly think he's happy living in a tiny area alone? I don't think so. I don't think you even care about her or her health. You just want the profites. I wish you knew what it would feel like to be taken from your family and put into a small area. Also with no one to be with but some strangers. You would probably be thinking of your family all the time. Whales were born to swim with their families and stay with their mothers. Not taken away and having to live with someone else. They probably don't enjoy doing a show for people and then a couple minutes later doing it over again. And over and over and over again. I personally don't think any whale would enjoy living like that.

I hope you know about whales skin. If it's out in the sun too much they get skin cancer. Or a disease. Corky has shows put on that make him come out of the water(i supose). Well, that will give her skin problems. I'm not saying you did'nt know but if you did I hope you will either let her free or leave her IN the water untill she is cured. Then, let her free.

PLEASE, PLEASE, PLEASE FREE CORKY !!!!!!!!!!!!!!!!!!!!!! MAKE HER HAPPY AND ALL THE OTHERS, INCLUDING ME, HAPPY. PLEASE PLEASE PLEASE PLEASE PLEASE PLEASE

Sincerely,
Tiffany Mayne

Ikaika

August 25, 2002
Born at SeaWorld Orlando

November 2006
Sent to Marineland Ontario

November 2011
Sent to SeaWorld San Diego

Species: Orcinus orca

Breed: 100% Icelandic

Meaning of name: Hawaiian for "strong"

Captivity history: Born in SeaWorld Orlando

Mother: Katina

Father: Tilikum

Full Siblings: Taku, Unna, Makaio

Offspring: None

Sex: Male

Weight: 7,200 lbs.

Length: 19 ft.

Photo courtesy of Samantha Cornwall (Instagram @samcorn.swo)

When Ikaika was in Ontario, SeaWorld took Marineland to court accusing them of not meeting SeaWorld's veterinary care. SeaWorld won the case and Ikaika was sent to SeaWorld San Diego.

In August of 2012, Ikaika was seen with a large gash on his chin presumably from the metal barriers that trainers use. He has mouthed trainers on several occasions.

Kalia

December 21, 2004
Born at SeaWorld San Diego

Species: Orcinus orca

Breed: 87.5% Icelandic, 12.5% Southern Resident

Meaning of name: Hawaiian for "beauty"

Captivity history: Born in SeaWorld San Diego

Mother: Kasatka

Father: Keet

Offspring: Amaya (2014)

Sex: Female

Weight: 4,600 lbs.

Length: 16 ft.

Trainers at SeaWorld San Diego putting a scope down Kalia's throat
August 5, 2015
Photo courtesy of Anonymous

Kalia became ill at six months old, was given daily injections for five weeks and had blood drawn every couple of days during the same period.

Kalia was artificially inseminated in 2012 at the age of 8 using Ulises's sperm. In November of 2014, a pregnant Kalia got stuck in one of the gates for about three minutes before the gate was opened. SeaWorld employees shrugged the incident off as Kalia "playing with the gate".

On December 2, 2014 Kalia gave birth to her first calf Amaya. Kalia often will regurgitate fish in order to bait birds, which, she learned from Nakai.

* Endoscopes are often used to check the GI tract of whales suspected of swallowing foreign objects (paint strips, toys, etc)

Keet

February 2, 1993	November 1999	1999	February 2001	April 2004	February 2012
Born at SW San Antonio	Sent to San Diego	Sent to Ohio	Sent to San Diego	Sent to San Antonio	Sent to San Diego

Species: Orcinus orca

Breed: 75% Icelandic, 25% Southern Resident

Meaning of name: Tlingit for "Orca"

Captivity history: Born at SeaWorld San Antonio

Mother: Kalina

Father: Kotar

Full Siblings: Keto

Offspring: Kalia (2004), Halyn (2005)

Sex: Male

Weight: 8,000 lbs.

Length: 19 ft.

Keet on right
SeaWorld San Diego
Photo courtesy of PETA

When Keet was only a year old, his mother was moved away from him. Being the sub-dominant whale, he has been raked by other whales causing him to shiver.

At SeaWorld San Diego he swallowed a ball and pole when it was left in the pool. Keet seems to have something wrong with his dorsal fin,but no one has clarified what exactly it is, perhaps other whales chewing on him or a possible disease.

Makani

February 14, 2013
Born at SeaWorld San Diego

Species: Orcinus orca

Breed: 50% Icelandic; 50% Argentinian Transient

Meaning of name: Hawaiian for "wind"

Captivity history: Born at SeaWorld San Diego

Mother: Kasatka

Father: Kshamenk

Full Siblings: None

Offspring: None

Sex: Male

Weight: 2,700 lbs.

Length: 13 ft.

Makani at SeaWorld San Diego on August 5, 2015 getting "enrichment" time with trainer.
Photo courtesy of Anonymous.

Makani was conceived through artificial insemination.

At just four years old, Makani's mother Kasatka passed away.

After her passing, Makani could been seen with numerous rake marks.

Nakai

September 1, 2001
Born at SeaWorld San Diego

Species: Orcinus orca
Breed: 100% Icelandic
Meaning of name: Native American for "victory"
Captivity history: Born at SeaWorld San Diego
Mother: Kasatka
Father: Tilikum
Offspring: None
Sex: Male
Weight: 7,000 lbs.
Length: 18 ft.

Photo courtesy of Samantha Cornwall (Instagram @ samcorn.swo)

Nakai was the first Orca to be successfully conceived through artificial insemination.

He was born headfirst which is rare since Orcas need air to breathe.

On September 20, 2012 Nakai lost a large chunk of flesh under his chin during a nighttime show. No one can confirm how this happened. People speculate it was either an injury from an altercation between Nakai, Keet, and Ikaika or from scraping a metal railing.

Nakai with rake marks SeaWorld San Diego Photo courtesy of Elizabeth

Nakai will often regurgitate fish in order to bait birds as a way to entertain himself.

Orkid

September 23, 1988
Born at SeaWorld San Diego

Species: Orcinus orca
Breed: Hybrid - 50% Icelandic, 50% Northern
Resident
Meaning of name: After father Orky, "Orky's kid"
Captivity history: Born at SeaWorld San Diego
Mother: Kandu V
Father: Orky II
Offspring: None, although several attemps were made to artificially inseminate her
Sex: Female
Weight: 6,100 lbs.
Length: 19 ft.

Photo courtesy of Sara Farrell

Orkid's father died shortly after her birth and her mother died in 1989 after ramming into Corky. Corky then became a surrogate mother to Orkid. Orkid has been involved in over fifteen human aggression incidents at SeaWorld.

A few notable incidents were in 2002 when Orkid grabbed trainer Tamaree's leg and pulled her into the pool. Three years later, she dunked a trainer and a year after that, she grabbed a trainer by the foot. In 2007, Orkid sent another trainer to the hospital by knocking her over a wall. Orkid has pulled trainers to the bottom of her pool on several occasions. Losing her mother at only 11 months old could be the root of her aggression, but no one can know for sure.

Shouka

February 25, 1993
Born at Marineland Antibes

May 2002
Sent to Six Flags Ohio

April 2004
Sent to Six Flags California

August 2012
Sent to SeaWorld San Diego

Species: Orcinus orca
Breed: 100% Icelandic
Meaning of name: Inuit for "beautiful one"
Captivity history: Born at Marineland Antibes, France
Mother: Sharkan
Father: Kim II
Full Siblings: Inouk, Wikie
Offspring: None
Sex: Female
Weight: 5,000 lbs.
Length: 17 ft.

Shouka was the first Orca born in captivity in Europe. For fear she would mate with her father, she was moved to Ohio at the age of 9.

Shouka was housed alone while in Ohio and only in California was a dolphin introduced to her tank. After ten years of not seeing another Orca, she was finally moved to San Diego where she is now housed with nine other whales.

In July of 2012, Shouka lunged out of the pool at a trainer, but since then there have been no incidents with Shouka, many people believe that her incident was simply a result of her being kept alone for so many years.

Photo courtesy of Heather Jordan

Ulises

1977 est	November 1980	Nov-Dec 1980	Dec 1980-June 1983	June 1983-Jan 1994	1994
Born	Captured Iceland	Sædyrasafnid Aquarium	Sent to Rioleón Safari	Sent to Barcelona Zoo	Sent to SW Diego

Species: Orcinus orca
Breed: 100% Icelandic
Meaning of name: Latin for "wrathful"
Captivity history: Captured from Reyðarfjörður, Iceland at age 3
Offspring: Moana (2011), Amaya (2014)
Sex: Male
Weight: 9,570 lbs.
Length: 21 ft.

Photo courtesy of Samanta Cornwall

Ulises is the oldest male Orca in captivity. He is the largest Orca in captivity now that Tilikum has passed away.

He was in captivity for the first thirteen years of his life alone before he was sent to SeaWorld San Diego in 1994.

Wikie was artificially inseminated with Ulises sperm and gave birth to Moana in 2011.

Ulises came at a trainer in 1997 and pushed/blocked a trainer in SCUBA gear in 2004.

In 2007 Ulises lost most of his eyesight due to burns but has since recovered.

MIAMI SEAQUARIUM, FLORIDA, USA

Photo by Tiffany Humphrey

Founded: 1955

Housed Orcas Since: 1968

Location: Miami, Florida, USA

Dimensions:

Front Pool - 35 ft wide x 80 ft long x 18 ft deep

Back pool - 38 ft wide x 60 ft long x 10 ft deep

Orcas: 1 (Lolita)

Lolita

1966 est
Born

August 8, 1970
Captured in Penn Cove, WA

September 1970
Sold to Miami Seaquarium

Species: Orcinus orca
Breed: Southern Resident
Meaning of name: Spanish for "strong woman"
Captivity History: Captured at age 4 from L pod of Southern Residents in Penn Cove, WA
Mother: L25
Siblings: Tsunami
Offspring: No viable offspring
Sex: Female
Weight: 7,500 lbs.
Length: 20 ft.
Tank measurements:
80 ft wide. Horizontal dimension of 35 ft. Depth is 20 ft in the middle and 12 ft around the edges–it is the smallest tank in North America.

Lolita being captured in Penn Cove, WA 1970
Photo courtesy of Wallie Funk

Lolita is also referred to as Tokitae, which is Salish for "nice day". Lolita was housed with another Orca named Hugo, but ever since his death in 1980 Lolita has been alone at the Miami Seaquarium. She is one of the oldest Orcas in captivity. On February 4, 2015, Lolita was officially included in the endangered listing of the Southern Resident Orca Distinct Population Segment (DPS) by NMFS.

* See appendix for more photos of Lolita

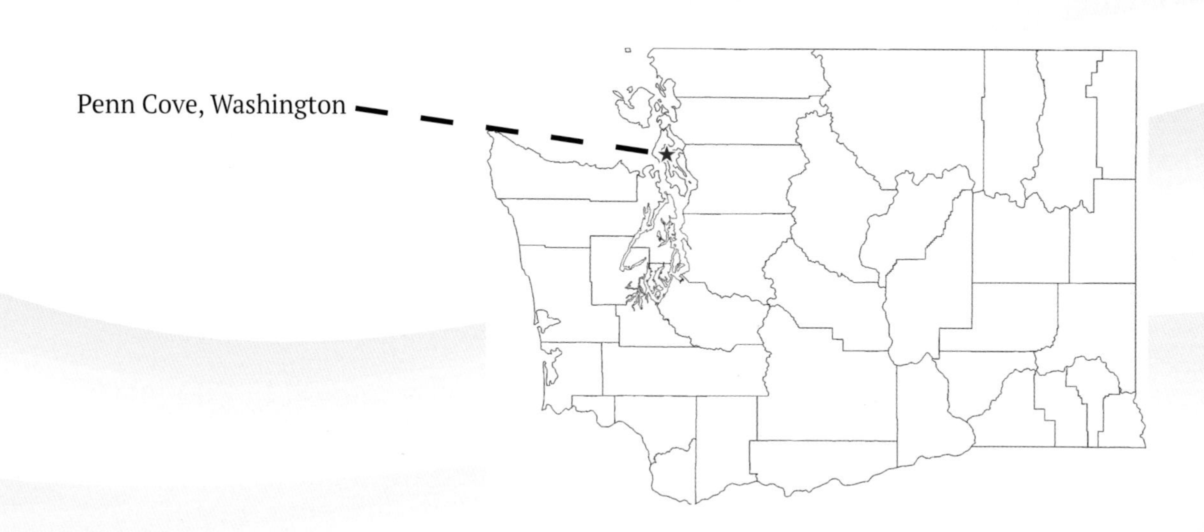

MARINELAND ANTIBES, FRANCE

Photo courtesy of Sea Shepherd Nice

Founded: 1970

Housed Orcas Since: 1969

Location: Antibes, France

Dimensions: 210 ft long x 100 ft wide x 40 ft deep

Water: 11M gallons

Orcas: 4 (Inouk, Keijo, Moana, Wikie)

** Major Flood damage in October 2015 resulted in the death of Valentin. In April 2016, Sea Shepherd France initiated a lawsuit against Marineland Antibes for negligence in not being prepared for a catastrophic flood event on a flood plain.

Inouk

February 23, 1999
Born at Marineland Antibes, France

Species: Orcinus orca

Breed: 100% Icelandic

Meaning of name: Inuit for "person"

Captivity History: Born in Marineland Antibes

Mother: Sharkane

Father: Kim II

Full Siblings: Shouka, Wikie

Offspring: None

Sex: Male

Weight: 6,200 lbs.

Length: 17 ft.

Young Inouk, Marineland Antibes
Photo courtesy of Stefan Jacobs
www.Orcahome.de

Inouk 's father died in 2005 and his mother died in 2009, when Inouk was only 10 years old.

His dorsal fin is completely collapsed to the right side and after gnawing on the pool walls in boredom for two decades, has worn his teeth down to the pulp.

Keijo

November 20, 2013
Born at Marineland Antibes, France

Species: Orcinus orca
Breed: 100% Icelandic
Meaning of name: Finnish for "supernatural being"
Captivity History: Born at Marineland Antibes
Mother: Wikie
Father: Valentin
Offspring: None
Sex: Male
Weight: 350 lbs.
Length: 7 ft.

Photo courtesy of Hah

Keijo is inbred because Kim II is his grandfather on both his mother and his father's side. His parents, Wikie and Valentin, were half-brother and half-sister.

He has been observed banging on the windows.

As a result of the flood in 2015, Valentin died at just nineteen years old, which undoubtedly left a mark on Keijo and the other Orcas in the park who witnessed the tragedy.

Moana

March 16, 2011
Born at Marineland Antibes, France

Species: Orcinus orca

Breed: 100% Icelandic

Meaning of name: Polynesian for "ocean"

Captivity History: Born in Marineland Antibes

Mother: Wikie

Father: Ulises

Offspring: None

Sex: Male

Weight: 1,800 lbs.

Length: 11.5 ft.

Moana was the third calf artificially conceived worldwide, and the first calf in Europe conceived and born through artificial insemination.

Marineland Antibes
Photo courtesy of Sea Shepherd Nice

Wikie

June 1, 2001
Born at Marineland Antibes, France

Species: Orcinus orca

Breed: 100% Icelandic

Meaning of name: Hawaiian for "fast"

Captivity History: Born in Marineland Antibes

Mother: Sharkane

Father: Kim II

Full Siblings: Shouka, Inouk

Offspring: Moana (2011), Keijo (2013)

Sex: Female

Weight: 4,500 lbs.

Length: 17.1 ft.

Marineland Antibes
Photo courtesy of Stefan Jacobs
www.Orcahome.de

In 2009, using Ulises' semen, Wikie was the youngest Orca to be artificially inseminated.

In 2009 she pushed a trainer underwater and after other small infractions, all water-works with her were stopped.

In 2018, Wikie became the first Orca recorded saying human phrases such as hello, bye-bye, and one-two-three.

MARINELAND, CANADA

Photo by Tiffany Humphrey

Founded: 1961

Housed Orcas Since: 1972

Location: Ontario, Canada

Dimensions: A, B, C – Kiska is allowed in Pools B + C (medical pool)

Water: Marineland won't release the data on their pool dimensions or water capacity

Orcas: 1 (Kiska)

*May 2015 – The Ontario Society for the Prevention of Cruelty to Animals Amendment Act, which prohibits the acquisition and breeding of Orcas in Ontario was passed.

Kiska

1976 est Born	Fall 1979 Captured in Ingolfshofdi, Iceland	November – December 1979 Held at Sædyrasafnid Aquarium	December 1979 Sent to Marineland Ontario

Species: Orcinus orca
Breed: 100% Icelandic
Meaning of name: Russian for "pure"
Captivity History: Captured at the age of 3 in Iceland
Offspring: Unnamed calf, Kanuck, Nova, Hudson, Athena
Sex: Female
Weight: 6,500 lbs.
Length: 20 ft.

Kiska currently resides alone at Marineland, Canada.

All five of Kiska's calves died before the age of 7. MLC-00-B9201 died at 2 months of age, Kanuck died at age 4, Nova died at age 4, Hudson died at age 6, and Athena died at age 4.

Marineland Ontario May 31, 2014
Photo courtesy of Jessica Shvimer

MUNDO MARINO, ARGENTINA, SOUTH AMERICA

Photo courtesy of Joel Rojas

Founded: 1978

Held Orcas Since: 1985

Location: Buenos Aires, Argentina

Dimensions:

Show Pool – 114 ft diameter x 21 ft deep; 449k gallons

Side Pools – 39 ft diameter x 9 ft deep

Orcas: 1 (Kshamenk)

Kshamenk

1988 est
Born

September 19, 1992
Captured in Samborombon Bay, Argentina

September 21, 1992
Moved to Mundo Marino

Species: Orcinus orca
Breed: 100% Argentinian Transient
Meaning of name: Yamana for "Orca"
Captivity history: Caught at the age of around 3 or 4 in Samborombon Bay, Argentina
Offspring: Balen's stillborn (1998), Belen's fetus (2000), Makani (2013), Kamea (2013)
Sex: Male
Weight: 7,800 lbs.
Length: 19.5 ft.

Photo courtesy of Sea Shepherd

It is uncertain how Kshamenk was brought into captivity. Mundo Marino claims that he was stranded along with three other Orcas, but eyewitnesses say they were forced to strand.

Kshamenk, the only survivor of the stranding, was taken to Mundo Marino and joined a female Orca named Belen. Belen and Kshamenk mated, but Belen delivered a still-born in 1998. Belen died in 2000 at the age of 13 while pregnant with a 4-month-old fetus. Kshamenk has been alone ever since, only sharing the pools with bottlenose dolphins.

SeaWorld traveled to Mundo Marino to get semen from Kshamenk and successfully artificially inseminated Kasatka and Takara.

LORO PARQUE, SPAIN

Photo courtesy of Britta Lenzner

Founded: 1972
Held Orcas Since: 2006 when SeaWorld sent Kohana, Tekoa, Ket and Skyla on a "breeding loan"
Location: Tenerife, Spain (Canary Islands)
Dimensions:
Show Pool – 395 ft long x 39 ft deep; 7M gallons
Side Pools - Not published

Orcas: 7 (Adan, Keto, Kohana, Morgan, Skyla, Tekoa, Ula)
* Metflex coating was improperly applied to the pool walls and the whales began eating stripes of the contaminant. A month after the shows began they were shut down while the pool walls could be fixed.

Adán

October 13, 2010
Born at Loro Parque, Spain

Species: Orcinus orca
Breed: 87.5% Icelandic, 12.5 % Southern Resident
Meaning of name: Spanish for "first man"
Captivity history: Born at Loro Parque
Mother: Kohana
Father: Keto
Full Siblings: Victoria
Offspring: None
Sex: Male
Weight: 3,000 lbs.
Length: 14.1 ft.

Kohana's mother Takara is Keto's half sister, making Adán slightly inbred. Adán was the first Orca to be born in captivity in Spain. Kohana did not take any interest in Adán when he was born and so trainers had to help raise him. Kohana was only 6 years old when she gave birth to Adán.

Adán's sister Victoria was born in 2012, but died in 2013 of intestinal complications.

Loro Parque
Photo courtesy of PETA

Keto

June 17, 1995
Born at SW Orlando

March 8, 1999
Sent to SW San Diego

April 15, 2000
Sent to SW Ohio

2001
Sent to SW San Antonio

February 13, 2006
Sent to Loro Parque, Spain

Species: Orcinus orca
Breed: 75% Icelandic, 25% Southern Resident
Meaning of name: Greek for "sea monster"
Captivity history: Born at SeaWorld Orlando
Mother: Kalina
Father: Kotar
Full Siblings: Keet
Offspring: Adan (2010), Victoria (2012)
Sex: Male
Weight: 8,000 lbs.
Length: 20.5 ft.

Keto was born at SeaWorld Orlando and at the age of three he pushed a trainer around the pool with his mouth open. At age 3 ½ he was taken from his mother and shipped to SeaWorld San Diego. In San Diego, he swam into a trainer with his mouth open and later the same year he snapped at a trainer.

After a year, he was shipped to SeaWorld Ohio and in 2001 he was shipped to San Antonio. In 2002, at SeaWorld San Antonio he swam into a trainer again with his mouth open. Keto was moved between all four SeaWorld parks before being shipped to the Canary Islands in 2006 where he currently resides. In the summer of 2007, Keto rammed into Tekoa at Loro Parque. On December 24, 2009 Keto rammed into his trainer Alexis Martinez killing him, see chapter 2: The Famous for more details.

Loro Parque
Photo courtesy of Britta Lenzner

Kohana

May 3, 2002
Born at SeaWorld San Diego

2004
Sent to SeaWorld Orlando

2006
Sent to Loro Parque, Spain

Species: Orcinus orca
Breed: 100% Icelandic
Meaning of name: Sioux for "swift"
Captivity history: Born at SeaWorld San Diego
Mother: Takara
Father: Tilikum
Full Siblings: Sakari
Offspring: Adan (2010), Victoria (2012)
Sex: Female
Weight: 5,000 lbs.
Length: 17 ft.

Kohana was the second Orca to be born from artificial insemination. Kohana and her mother Takara were moved together to SeaWorld Orlando when Kohana was 2.

At the age of 4, Kohana was taken from her mother and shipped to Loro Parque in the Canary Islands. At only 8 years old, Kohana gave birth to Adan who is still at Loro Parque with her. In 2012, Kohana gave birth to her second calf Victoria, who died one year later of intestinal complications.

Kohana at Loro Parque
Photo courtesy of Britta Lenzner

Morgan

2007 est
Born

June 23, 2010
Captured in Wadden Sea

November 29, 2001
Sent to Loro Parque, Spain

Species: Orcinus orca
Breed: 100% Norwegian
Meaning of name: Celtic for "inhabitants of the sea"
Captivity history: Captured in the Wadden Sea, Netherlands from P Pod at age 3
Offspring: None
Sex: Female
Weight: 5,000 lbs.
Length: 17 ft.

At age 3, Morgan was taken by the Dolfinarium Harderwijk under a "rescue, rehabilitation and release" Dutch government permit. Although Morgan was found to be emaciated, she was not stranded or in danger when taken. Eighteen months later she was shipped to Loro Parque.

Wolfgang Kiessling, owner of Loro Parque was quoted in a newspaper saying Morgan was sent to them as a "donation from nature" and a "new blood line" for breeding.

On April 27, 2016 a video was released online showing Morgan repeatedly ramming into the gate of the medical pool while Tekoa looked on from the adjacent pool.

Morgan is said to be partially deaf.

Skyla

February 9, 2004
Born at SeaWorld Orlando

2006
Sent to Loro Parque, Spain

Species: Orcinus orca
Breed: 75% Icelandic, 25% Southern Resident
Meaning of name: Celtic for "learned one"
Captivity history: Born at SeaWorld Orlando
Mother: Kalina
Father: Tilikum
Full Siblings: Tuar
Offspring: None
Sex: Female
Weight: 4,500 lbs.
Length: 18 ft.

Skyla, born at SeaWorld Orlando, was separated from her mother at the age of two and shipped to Loro Parque. Her mother Kalina repeatedly rammed the gate when they took her daughter from her.

In 2009, Skyla pushed her trainer Rafa Sanchez around the pool and into the pool wall.

Special protocols were enacted with Skyla regarding waterworks after this incident.

Skyla can be seen with rake marks inflicted upon her by another female at Loro Parque named Kohana.

Loro Parque
Photo courtesy of PETA

Tekoa

November 8, 2000
Born at SeaWorld Orlando

April 2004
Sent to SeaWorld San Antonio

February 13, 2006
Sent to Loro Parque, Spain

Species: Orcinus orca
Breed: 75% Icelandic, 25% Bigg's Transient
Meaning of name: Cherokee for "beautiful"
Captivity history: Born at SeaWorld Orlando
Mother: Taima
Father: Tilikum
Full Siblings: Malia, Sumar
Offspring: None
Sex: Male
Weight: 5,800 lbs.
Length: 18 ft.

Tekoa was born at SeaWorld Orlando to mother Taima. Taima was aggressive towards Tekoa and so they were permanently separated from each other. In the summer of 2007, Keto aggressively rammed into Tekoa at Loro Parque. On October 6, 2007 Tekoa grabbed the arm of his trainer Claudia Vollhardt and pulled her to the bottom of the pool. He then pushed her up against the gate between the pools. Claudia was pulled from the water, sustaining a punctured lung and fractured forearm.

Waterworks at Loro Parque were discontinued for six months and no trainers were allowed to get into the water with Tekoa again.

Loro Parque
Photo courtesy of PETA

Ula

September 22, 2018
Born at Loro Parque, Spain

Species: Orcinus orca
Breed: 50% Norwegian, 37.5% Icelandic, 12.5 % Southern Resident
Meaning of name: Celtic for “gem of the sea”
Captivity history: Born at Loro Parque
Mother: Morgan
Father: Keto
Sex: Female
Weight: 1,100 lbs.
Length: 7 ft.

In 2016, SeaWorld announced they were ending their breeding program. SeaWorld and Loro Parque are in partnership with one another. In September of 2018, Ula (oo-lah) was born at Loro Parque. She was born with a melon deformity and at only five months old was seen with several skin infections on her pectoral fin and tail.

Ula on right

KAMOGAWA SEAWORLD, JAPAN

Photo courtesy of Anonymous

Founded: 1970

Held Orcas Since: 1970

Location: Chiba, Japan

Dimensions:

Show Pool – 102 ft long x 65 ft wide x 21 ft deep; 924k gallons water

Back Pool – 60 ft long x 42 ft wide x 15 ft deep; 343k gallons water

Orcas: 4 (Lara, Lovey, Luna, Ran II)

*** This is the only park in the world that still allows trainers in the water with the Orcas

Lara

February 8, 2001
Born at Kamogawa SeaWorld

Species: Orcinus orca

Breed: 100% Icelandic

Meaning of name: Russian for “cheerful”

Captivity history: Born at Kamogawa SeaWorld

Mother: Stella

Father: Bingo

Full Siblings: Lovey, Sarah, Ran II and Rin

Offspring: None

Sex: Female

Weight: 4,850 lbs.

Length: 17.3 ft.

Photo courtesy of Hah

Lara lives at Kamogawa SeaWorld along with her sisters Ran II and Lovey. She was the second Orca born in captivity in Japan. Her mother Stella was taken away from her when she was only ten years old and sent to Port of Nagoya. In 2015, Lara was being trained for artificial insemination.

Lovey

January 11, 1998
Born at Kamogawa SeaWorld, Japan

Species: Orcinus orca

Breed: 100% Icelandic

Meaning of name: English for “loved one”

Captivity history: Born at Kamogawa SeaWorld

Mother: Stella

Father: Bingo

Full Siblings: Lara, Sarah, Rann II, Rin

Offspring: Earth (2008), Luna (2012)

Sex: Female

Weight: 4,850 lbs.

Length: 16.7 ft.

Photo courtesy of Hah

Lovey was the first Orca successfully born at Kamogawa SeaWorld. Her stage name was Oyako before the name Lovey was picked.

In 2011 Lovey’s mother Stella was moved to Port of Nagoya.

Lovey gave birth to her first calf Earth in 2008. Earth would play rough with his sister Luna and was soon sent to the back of the pool so that Lovey wouldn’t displace Earth for his behavior. Earth was sent to Port of Nagoya in 2015. Lovey’s daughter Luna still resides with her as well as her sisters Lara and Ran II.

Luna

July 19, 2012
Born at Kamogawa SeaWorld

Species: Orcinus orca

Breed: 100% Icelandic

Meaning of name: Latin for "moon"

Captivity history: Born at Kamogawa SeaWorld

Mother: Lovey

Father: Oscar

Full Siblings: Earth

Offspring: None

Sex: Female

Weight: 620 lbs.

Length: 9 ft.

Photo courtesy of Hah

Luna was born at Kamogawa SeaWorld to mother Lovey and father Oscar. Her father Oscar died five months after she was born.

Her brother Earth would often times play rough with her and so they separated the two. Earth was eventually moved to Port of Nagoya.

Luna currently lives with her mother Lovey. She is currently the youngest Orca at Kamogawa.

Ran II

February 25, 2006
Born at Kamogawa SeaWorld

December 2011
Sent to Port of Nagoya

December 2015
Sent to Kamogawa SeaWorld

Species: Orcinus orca

Breed: 100% Icelandic

Meaning of name: Japanese for "orchid"

Captivity history: Born at Kamogawa SeaWorld

Mother: Stella

Father: Bingo

Full Siblings: Lovey, Lara, Sarah, Rin

Offspring: None

Sex: Female

Weight: 3,750 lbs.

Length: 16.1 ft.

Lynn and Ran II
Photo courtesy of Hah

Ran II was born head first at Kamogawa SeaWorld to mother Stella and father Bingo. In 2011, Ran II along with her mother and father were moved to Port of Nagoya, Japan. In December of 2015, Ran II was shipped back to Kamogawa SeaWorld leaving her parents behind at Port of Nagoya.

She currently lives with her sisters Lovey and Lara. Ran II was being prepared for artificial insemination training back in 2016.

PORT OF NAGOYA, JAPAN

Founded: 1992
Held Orcas Since: 2003
Location: Nagoya, Japan
Dimensions:
Show Pool – 195 ft long x 98 ft wide x 39 ft deep
Back Pool – 39 ft deep
Back Pool – 39 ft deep
Orcas: 3 (Earth, Stella, Rin/Lynn)

Earth

October 13, 2008
Born at Kamogawa SeaWorld, Japan

December 7, 2015
Sent to Port of Nagoya Aquarium, Japan

Species: Orcinus orca
Breed: 100% Icelandic
Meaning of name: English for "ground"
Captivity history: Born at Kamogawa SeaWorld
Mother: Lovey
Father: Oscar
Full Siblings: Luna
Offspring: None
Sex: Male
Weight: 2,865 lbs.
Length: 14.1 ft.

Earth was born in 2008 at Kamogawa SeaWorld in Japan. When his sister Luna was born in 2012, his mother Lovey began to rake him aggressively.

Earth was then moved to the back pool with his father Oscar who died that same year of unknown causes. Earth remained in the back pool for two years before being sent to Port of Nagoya Aquarium on December 7, 2015.

Stella

1986 est	October 1987	December 1987	2011
Born	Captured in Iceland	Sent to Kamogawa SeaWorld, Japan	Sent to Port of Nagoya Aquarium

Species: Orcinus orca

Breed: 100% Icelandic

Meaning of name: Latin for "star"

Captivity history: Captured at age 1 from

Seydisfjördur, Iceland

Offspring: Lovey (1998), Lara (2001), Sarah (2003), Ran II (2006), Rin (2012)

Sex: Female

Weight: 4,850 lbs.

Length: 17 ft.

Photo courtesy of Hah

Stella was captured at the age of 1 in Seydisfjördur, Iceland. She was sent to Kamogawa SeaWorld a few months later where she remained for 24 years.

In 2011, Stella was moved to Port of Nagoya Aquarium and separated from her three calves, Lovey, Lara and Ran II. She is currently being held with one of her calves, Rin.

Rin/Lynn

November 13, 2012
Born at Port of Nagoya Aquarium, Japan

Species: Orcinus orca

Breed: 100% Icelandic

Meaning of name: Japanese for "cold"

Captivity history: Born at Port of Nagoya Aquarium

Mother: Stella

Father: Bingo

Full Siblings: Lovey, Lara, Sarah, Ran II

Offspring:

Sex: Female

Weight: 2,645 lbs.

Length: 13 ft.

Photo courtesy of Hah

Rin was born head first on November 13, 2012 at Port of Nagoya Aquarium, making her the first calf successfully born at that park.

In 2013 the public voted and changed her named to Lynn but you can still find both names being used.

Rin's mother Stella was sent to Port of Nagoya while she was pregnant with Rin, leaving her three other calves back in SeaWorld Kamogawa.

MOSKVARIUM, RUSSIA

Photo courtesy of Risha Fox

Founded: 1935

Held Orcas Since: 2013

Location: Moscow, Russia

Water: 25M liters

Orcas: 3 (Naja, Narnia, Nord)

Naja

2010 est
Born

July 2014
Captured from the Sea of Okhotsk , Russia

December 21, 2014
Sent to Moscow Dolphinarium

Species: Orcinus orca

Breed: 100% Russian

Meaning of names:

Naja is Arabic for “rescue”

Naya is Arabic for “renewal”

Malyshka is Russian for “little girl”

Captivity history: Captured at the age of 4 from Russia

Sex: Female

Weight: 4,960 lbs.

Length: 17 ft.

Photo courtesy of Risha Fox

The Russian Government issued a permit to capture ten Orcas for the entertainment industry and one of those Orcas captured was Naja, referred to sometimes as Malyshka or Juliet.

Naja was captured at the age of four from Russian waters and sent to the Moscow Dolphinarium, also called Moskvarium. Russian President Vladimir Putin attended the opening show at the Moskvarium.

The spelling “Naya” was added above as that is how it appears on the Moskvarium website when translated from Russian to English.

Narnia

2007 est	August 2012	2012	December 2013	December 2014
Born	Captured in Sea of Okhotsk, Russia	Sent to TINRO Center	Sent to VDNKh	Sent to Moscow Dolphinarium

Species: Orcinus orca

Breed: 100% Russian Transient

Meaning of name: Latin for “spring of water”

Captivity history: Captured at age 5 in Russian waters

Sex: Female

Weight: 7,000 lbs.

Length: 20 ft.

Photo courtesy of Risha Fox

Narnia was captured by the Sochi Dolphinarium in the Sea of Okhotsk at the age of 5. Plans were to have her perform for the Olympics, but after public outcry it was decided to not bring her to Sochi. She was held at the TINRO center in Nakhodka until December 2013.

She was then transferred to the VDNKh exhibition center, also known as the All-Russian Exhibition Center in Moscow, along with another Orca named Nord.

In December 2014 Narnia and Nord were shipped to the Moscow Dolphinarium where they reside with another Orca named Naja.

Nord

2009 est	October 2013	December 2013	December 2014
Born	Captured in the Sea of Okhotsk, Russia	Sent to VDNKh, Moscow	Sent to Moscow Dolphinarium

Species: Orcinus orca

Breed: 100% Russian

Meaning of name: Scandinavian for "north"

Captivity history: Captured in the Sea of Okhotsk, Russia

Sex: Male

Weight: 8,200 lbs.

Length: 22 ft.

Photo courtesy of Risha Fox

Nord was captured at the age of 4 from the Sea of Okhotsk in Russia and sent to the VDNKh exhibition center, also known as the All-Russian Exhibition Center in Moscow.

He was held here along with another Orca named Narnia. Nord and Narnia were then shipped to the Moscow Dolphinarium (Moskvarium) in December 2014 where they are currently held along with Naja.

SEASIDE DOLPHINARIUM, RUSSIA
aka "The Whale Jail"

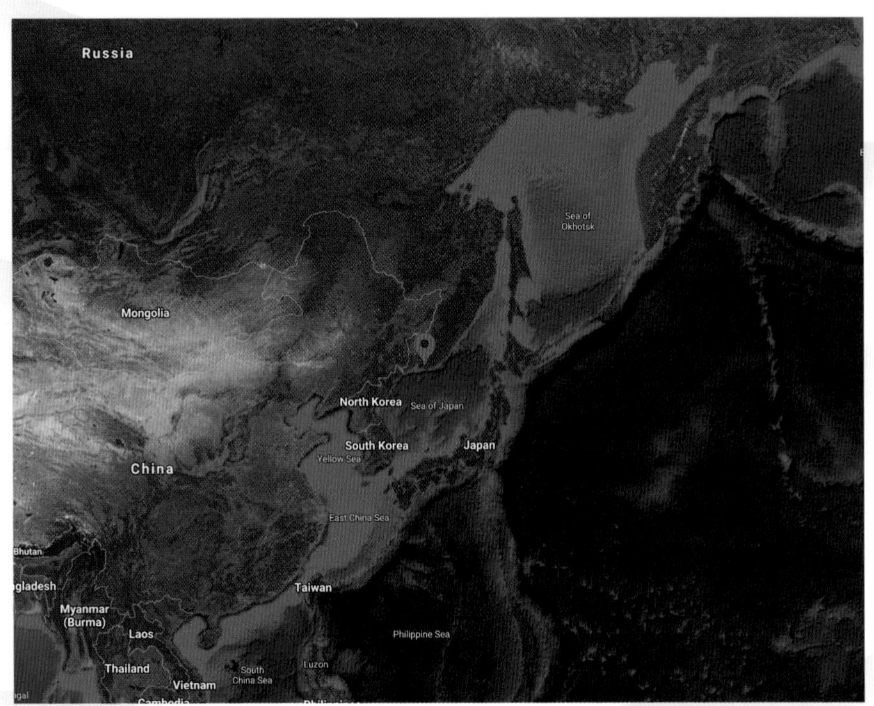

Imagery © 2020 Maxar Technologies, Map data © 2020 Google

Location: Srednyaya Bay, Nakhodka, Russia

In the summer of 2018, 11 Orcas and 87 beluga whales were captured in the seas off of Russia and transported to sea pens at the Dolphinarium, also referred to as the Center for the Adaptation of Marine Mammals. Although not much was known about the Orcas, at least two were given names; Leha and Kirill. In January 2019, an assessment of the Orcas noted their conditions were deteriorating. Leha had several skin injuries while Kirill was lethargic and breathing slow. The whales were kept in three small pens, a group of 3, a group of 4, and another group of 4. The Orcas were most likely transient mammal-eating whales, however, were being fed dead fish. After news got out that Kirill was no longer in the sea pen, the center claimed he had escaped. After public outcry, the Russian Federal Research Institute for Fisheries and Oceanography (VNIRO) began releasing all of the Orcas and belugas back to the Sea of Okhotsk, a process that was completed by November 2019. Two of the four companies guilty of obtaining the whales illegally have been fined - White Whale LLC was fined $435,000 and Oceanarium DV was fined $870,000.

Afalina LLC and Sochi Dolphinarium LLC will hopefully be fined as well.

At one time, the Dolphinarium held an Orca named Malvina, however, her location is unknown as of 2020.

Malvina

2012 est
Born

July 2015
Captured in the Sea of Okhotsk, Russia

2015
Sent to Seaside Dolphinarium Nakhodka

Species: Orcinus orca
Breed: 100% Russian Transient
Meaning of name: Irish for "sweet", Gaelic for "sweet brow"
Captivity history: Captured in Russia
Offspring: None
Sex: Female

Malvina was captured at the age of 3 by TINRO, the Russian Pacific Scientific Fisheries Center, from the Sea of Okhotsk in Russia.

She was moved to the Seaside Dolphinarium in Nakhodka where she was being held temporarily before being sold to a park. Malvina was housed with no other Orcas, only belugas and dolphins resided in nearby pens.

As of 2020, no information has been found regarding Malvina's current location or health status.

Sample photo
Photo & Location of Malvina Unknown

CHIMELONG OCEAN KINGDOM, CHINA

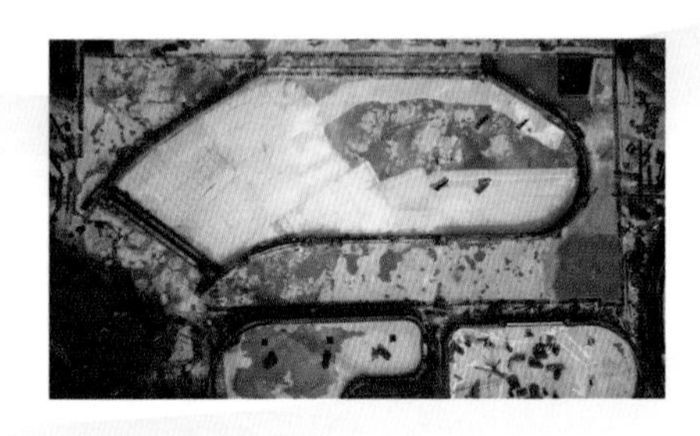

Photo courtesy of Anonymous

Founded: 2014

Location: Hengqin, Zhuhai,China

Orcas: 9 (Grace, Nukka, Orpheus, Tyson, 5 Unnamed)

Little is known about the Orcas at this facility. Between 2013-2015, these nine Orcas were captured in Russian waters. Their age, sex, and exact location of capture have not been published. There are 78 marine mammals parks in China and another 26 are currently under construction. An estimated 950 cetaceans are currently on display in the country.

SHANGHAI HAICHANG OCEAN PARK, CHINA

Photo courtesy of Anonymous

Founded: 2018
Location: Shanghai, China
Dimensions: Main tank 140 ft x 73 ft est
Orcas: 4 (Dora, Wow, Unknown female, Unknown male)

Dora (female)
Breed: Russian
Meaning of name: Greek for "gift"
Born: 2012 est
Dora was captured in the Sea of Okhotsk, Russia in 2015 when she was only three years old

Wow (Male)
Breed: Russian
Born: 2008 est
Wow was captured in the Sea of Okhotsk, Russia in 2014 when he was six years old

WUXI CHANGQIAO OCEAN KINGDOM, CHINA

Founded: 2019

Location: Hongshan, Wuxi, China

Orcas: 2 Unknown Orcas

CHAPTER 5: Blackfish

Blackfish is a documentary that has drastically changed the way much of the public view marine parks. Writer, producer and director Gabriela Cowperthwaite pulled back the proverbial curtain and gave viewers a look into the real life of captive whales at places such as SeaWorld. Gabriela began working on the film in 2010 after Dawn Brancheau's death and was released in 2013. The movie goes back in time and details how the Pacific Northwest Orcas were abducted and separated from their families in the early seventies. Original members of the capture team give their gruesome accounts of what went on during those horrific and sometimes deadly encounters. Tilikum's life of enslavement, however, is the focus of the movie first beginning with his mistreatment at Sealand of the Pacific and moving on to SeaWorld. Dawn Brancheau's death and subsequent lawsuit are highlighted as well as the deaths of Keltie Byrne, Daniel Dukes, and Alexis Martinez.

Directed by Gabriela Cowperthwaite

Produced by Manuel V. Oteyza, and Gabriela Cowperthwaite

Written by Gabriela Cowperthwaite, Eli Despres, and Tim Zimmermann

Music by Jeff Beal

Cinematography by Jonathan Ingalls and Christopher Towey

Edited by Eli Despres

Production companies CNN Films and Manny O. Productions

Distributed by Magnolia Pictures

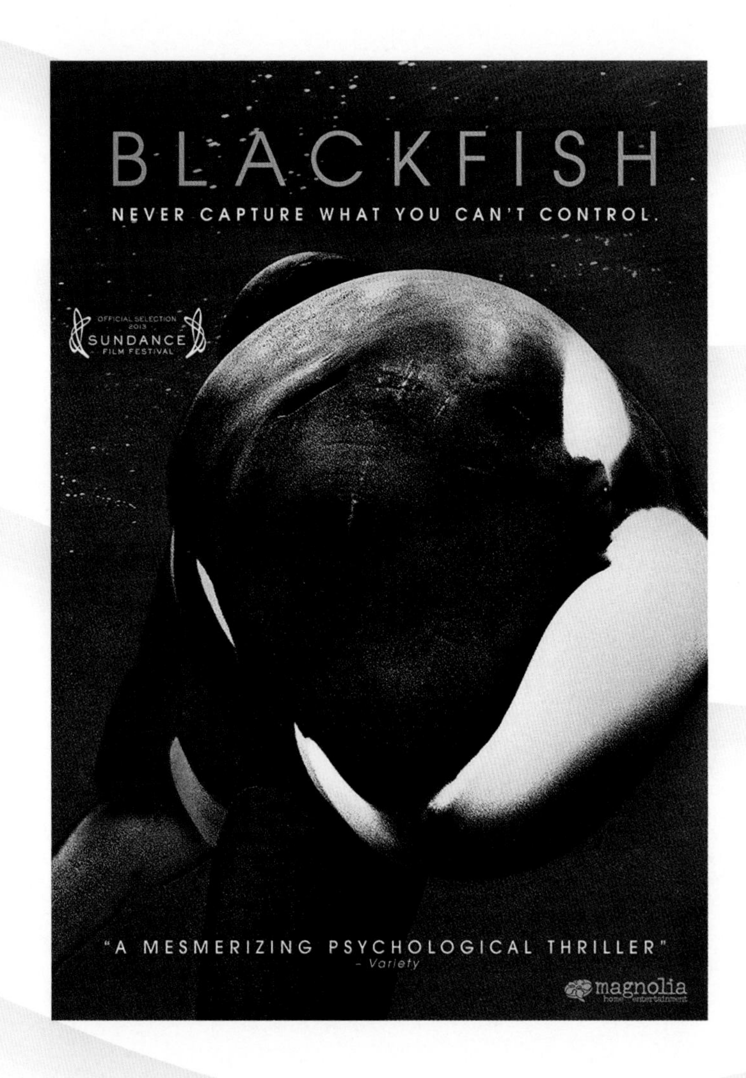
BLACKFISH
NEVER CAPTURE WHAT YOU CAN'T CONTROL.
OFFICIAL SELECTION 2013
SUNDANCE
FILM FESTIVAL
"A MESMERIZING PSYCHOLOGICAL THRILLER"
– Variety
magnolia
home entertainment

CHAPTER 6: The Advocates

These groups are working to protect and defend Orcas and working to shut down Orca prisons around the world

Sea Shepherd Conservation Society
Founded in 1977 by Captain Paul Watson to intervene against illegal activities exploiting marine wildlife.
Education, litigation, research and intervention.
https://seashepherd.org

Sea Shepherd France
Sea Shepherd France is focusing on shutting down Marineland in Antibes through education and litigation.
https://www.seashepherd.fr/

Orcalab
Founded in Canada in 1970 by Dr. Paul Spong. Orca conservation and research without interfering with their lives or habitat.
https://orcalab.org/

Dolphin Project
Founded by Ric O'Barry in 1970 with the mission to end dolphin exploitation and slaughter.
https://www.dolphinproject.com/

Orca Research Trust
Founded in 1998 by Dr. Ingrid Visser in New Zealand. Their mission is to protect Orcas and their habitats through conservation, education, and scientific research.
https://www.orcaresearch.org/

Oceanic Preservation Society
Founded in 2005 by Louie Psihoyos. Creating film and inspiring awareness through visual displays.
OPS produced the academy award winning film *The Cove*
https://www.opsociety.org/

Earth Island Institute
Founded by David Brower in 1982. EII freed Keiko from captivity in 2002.
https://www.earthisland.org/

Whale Sanctuary Project
Founded in 2016 by Lori Marino to develop marine sanctuaries for Orcas to facilitate their release to the wild.
www.whalesanctuaryproject.org

The sonar that allows free cetaceans to perceive the marine environment with extraordinary acuity is completely unsuited to the dreary environment of a smooth-surfaced tank that constantly reflects their visual and auditory image. It becomes a source of additional stress that augments the animals' boredom and depression. Sea Shepherd created the **Tilikum Tank**—the name pays homage to the orca that captivity turned into a killer and whose story is covered by the documentary Blackfish—to let people experience for themselves what captivity for these animals is like. The floor and walls are covered with mirrors, since everything the cetaceans perceive in their tiny underwater prisons is their own reflection and the constant echo of their own voices, superimposed over show music blasting at top volume. The public is invited to spend a few minutes in this "tank" to get a better idea. Pamela Anderson, who unveiled the Tilikum Tank in Cannes in May 2016, commented on her experience: "I couldn't stay in it even for the recommended three minutes, and when I got out, I wanted to bite someone. I can't imagine what hell it must be to spend your whole life under conditions like that."

Photo courtesy of Sea Shepherd France

CHAPTER 7: Alternatives

Sea Pens

Following the death of Dawn Brancheau, the Secretary of Labor took SeaWorld of Florida to court. The outcome of that OSHA hearing was a small fine and most notably that trainers were no longer allowed to perform waterworks in the tanks with the whales. The question this outcome raises is – what will SeaWorld do with these whales now?

Some have argued for the release of all captive whales, however, this is nearly impossible as most have drilled teeth making them prone to infection and in some cases incapable of catching fish. Some believe that the Orcas should remain in captivity but just not perform during shows.

We would like to propose a compromise to both suggestions. We believe that all of the captive Orcas deserve to live out the remainder of their lives in freedom and so a viable option would be sea pens. The Orcas would have the opportunity to be trained to catch fish, swim in natural ocean water and dive to deeper depths. SeaWorld trainers would still be on hand to assess their health and progress and customers could still be charged to enter the park and see the whales living a more natural life style.

No longer would the Orcas be deprived of food in order to perform tricks in a small pool of chlorinated water. No longer would they lay motionless at the surface with harmful UV rays penetrating their cornea and skin. Gelatin cubes would no longer be needed to supplement their water intake, as they would receive adequate amounts of water through eating live fish. Females would no longer be artificially inseminated and forced to reproduce every couple of years. Babies should remain with their mothers throughout the remainder of their lives and no longer shipped around the world forced into unnatural social structures. The longer the babies are around their mothers and relatives the more chance they have of growing into normal whales and not undisciplined rogue whales.

Sea pens would give the whales more room in order to avoid aggressive acts by other whales. No longer would sub-dominant males be forced into small holding pens with dominant females and raked repeatedly. If progress is shown in the sea pen rehabilitation process and the whereabouts of the captives' relatives are known, perhaps at that point in time a release would be a viable option for certain whales.

Whale Watching

Whale watching began in the 1950's when a fisherman took people out to see the gray whale migration. It has since turned into a $2+ billion global industry with over 13 million ecotourists enjoying the pastime each year. In 2009, the whale watching industry employed over 13,000 jobs and is set to add $400 million and 5,000 jobs annually to the economy. Whale watching is a great alternative to amusement parks and you can get an up close look at Orcas in their nature environment. Whale watching gives the tourists the opportunity to see how true pods interact with each other, listen on hydrophones of them communicating, watch them feed, play and perform natural behaviors rather than food deprived learned tricks. The whale watchers also have the pleasure of watching them swim off into the sunset rather than leaving a park guilt-stricken. There are some places to whale watch without having to board a boat. Lime Kiln Point State Park on the west side of San Juan Island, WA offers viewers an opportunity to watch Orcas swim right past the shore as they head through Haro Strait in search of Chinook salmon between May and October. If you are on San Juan Island you can also stop by the Whale Museum in the town of Friday Harbor to learn about the resident Orcas and listen to guest speakers talk about their research in the Puget Sound. Below is a list of the most common places to see Orcas. If you don't find an area close to you it does not mean there are not Orcas that can be seen on occasion. Orcas are found in all oceans of the world so chances are you can find them in the waters closest to you!

Canada
Victoria
Vancouver
Nova Scotia
Labrador
Newfoundland
Quebec

United States
Seward, Alaska
Bellingham, Washington
Everett, Washington
Anacortes, Washington
Seattle, Washington
San Juan Island, Washington
Depoe Bay, Oregon
Pacific City, Oregon
Newport, Oregon
Newport Beach, California
Monterey Bay, California
Santa Barbara, California
Marina Dey Ray, California
Redondo Beach, California
Long Beach, California
Dana Point, California
Hawaii

Caribbean
Dominica

South America
Valdes Peninsula, Argentina
Osa Peninsula, Costa Rica
Brunswick Peninsula, Chile

Africa
Cape Town, South Africa

Europe
Caithness, Scotland
Shetland Islands, Scotland
Orkney, Scotland
West Cork, Ireland
Algarve, Portugal
Azores, Portugal
Reykjavik, Iceland
Husavik, Iceland
Vestfjord, Norway
Tysfjord, Norway
Ofotfjord, Norway

Australia and New Zealand
Auckland, New Zealand
Wellington, New Zealand
Kaikoura, New Zealand
Western Australia, Australia
Eden, NSW, Australia
Bruny Island, Tasmania, Australia

Japan
Choshi

Other
Antarctica
Greenland
Bering Sea
Chukchi Sea
Barents Sea
Sea of Okhotsk
Sea of Japan

APPENDIX

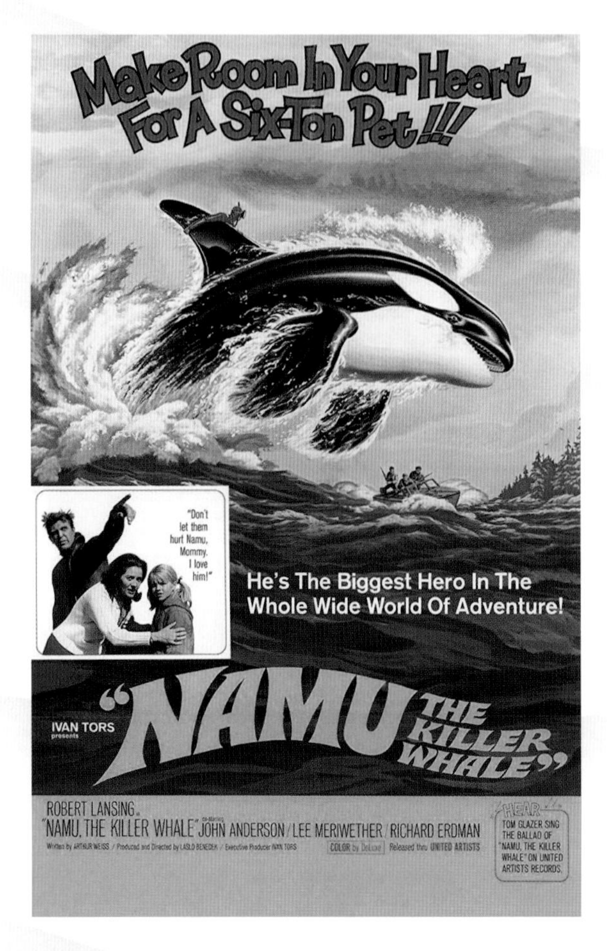

Poster from 1966 movie Namu, The Killer Whale

Killer Whales Destroyed

VP-7 Accomplishes Special Task

Adm. Jerauld Wright, Commander in Chief, Atlantic Fleet, has announced the completion of another successful mission by VP-7 against killer whales off the coast of Iceland.

Killer whales annually plague Icelandic fishermen by damaging and destroying thousands of dollars worth of fishing nets. Last year VP-18 destroyed hundreds of killer whales with machine guns, rockets and depth charges.

Before the Navy lent a hand last year, killer whales threatened to cut the Icelandic fish catch in half. This created a crisis because fishing employs about 20% of the population and accounts for the majority of Iceland's foreign currency income.

The Icelandic Office requested help, and Capt. W. A. Sherrill, Commander of the Naval Forces in Iceland, assigned VP-7 to the task of ridding the coastal areas of killer whales. Ranging from 20 to 30 feet in length, they are feared as one of the deadliest of ocean creatures.

19

Newspaper clipping from 1950s

"Enrichment" tools for the Orcas at SeaWorld San Diego August 5, 2016
Photo courtesy of Anonymous

Nakai and Kalia entertaining themselves
by playing with birds
Photo courtesy of Hah

Purse-seine net

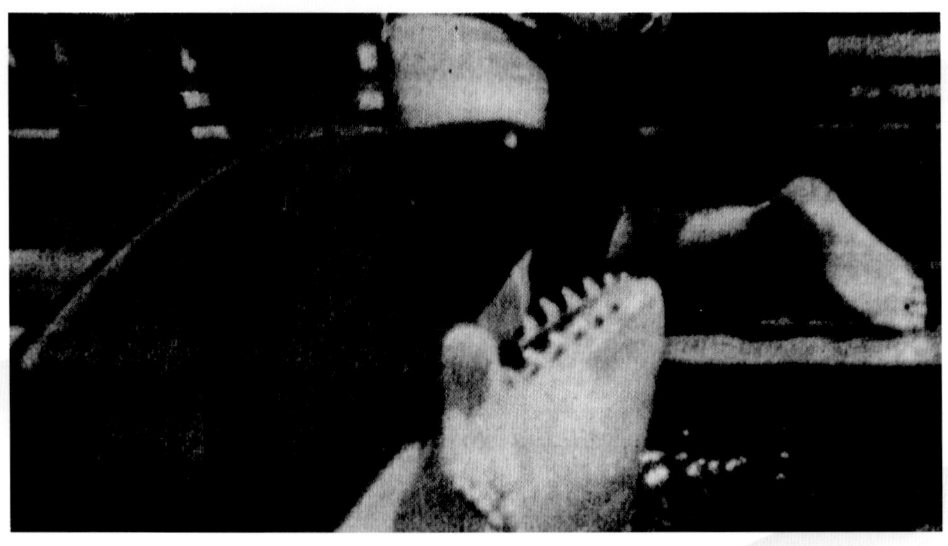

Shamu holding Annette Eckis' leg
The Sedalia Democrat Newspaper
April 21, 1971

Kiska with drilled/worn teeth
Marineland Canada
Photo by Tiffany Humphrey

Dental work being done on whale in background
SeaWorld San Diego
Photo courtesy of Elizabeth

Captain Paul Watson examining Haida II's teeth
at Marineland of the Pacific in Victoria, B.C. with daughter Lilliolani watching nearby
Photo by Captain Paul Watson

Marineland Canada
Photo by Tiffany Humphrey

Ulises with rake marks
Photo courtesy of Elizabeth

Title I—Conservation and Protection of Marine Mammals

Moratorium on taking and importing marine mammals and marine mammal products
16 U.S.C. 1371 Sec. 101.

(a) Imposition; exceptions There shall be a moratorium on the taking and importation of marine mammals and marine mammal products, commencing on the effective date of this chapter, during which time no permit may be issued for the taking of any marine mammal and no marine mammal or marine mammal product may be imported into the United States except in the following cases:

(1) Consistent with the provisions of section 1374 of this title, permits may be issued by the Secretary for taking, and importation for purposes of scientific research, public display, photography for educational or commercial purposes, or enhancing the survival or recovery of a species or stock, or for importation of polar bear parts (other than internal organs) taken in sport hunts in Canada. Such permits, except permits issued under section 1374 (c)(5) of this title, may be issued if the taking or importation proposed to be made is first reviewed by the Marine Mammal Commission and the Committee of Scientific Advisors on Marine Mammals established under subchapter III of this chapter. The Commission and Committee shall recommend any proposed taking or importation, other than importation under section 1374 (c)(5) of this title, which is consistent with the purposes and policies of section 1361 of this title. If the Secretary issues such a permit for importation, the Secretary shall issue to the importer concerned a certificate to that effect in such form as the Secretary of the Treasury prescribes, and such importation may be made upon presentation of the certificate to the customs officer concerned.

Sources

Ellis, Richard. Men and Whales

Ford, J., Ellis, G., Balcomb, K. Killer Whales second edition

Hargrove, John. Beneath the Surface

Hoyt, Erich. Orca, the Whale Called Killer

Kirby, David. Death at SeaWorld

Knudtson, Peter. Orca; Visions of the Killer Whale

Neiwert, David. Of Orcas and Men; What Killer Whales Can Teach Us

Obee, B., Ellis, G. Guardians of the Whales

Perrin, W., Wursig, B., Thewissen, J. Encyclopedia of Marine Mammals, Second Edition

Pollard, Sandra. Puget Sound Whales for Sale; The Fight to End Orca Hunting

http://Orcahome.de/

http://Orcapod.wikia.com/wiki/

www.ceteceancousin.com

http://www.Orcanetwork.org/

https://theOrcaproject.wordpress.com/

Blackfish (2013)

Southern Resident Orca
Photo by Tiffany Humphrey

About the Authors

Captain Paul Watson is a Canadian/American marine conservation activist, who founded the direct-action group Sea Shepherd Conservation Society in 1977. He has been described as "the world's most aggressive, most determined, most active and most effective defender of wildlife."

Tiffany Humphrey has been working with marine wildlife since 2003 in South Carolina, Washington, and Hawaii. From 2009-2013 she worked as Paul's Executive Assistant at Sea Shepherd Conservation Society. She lives with her husband Charlie and two children, Jacob, and Emily.

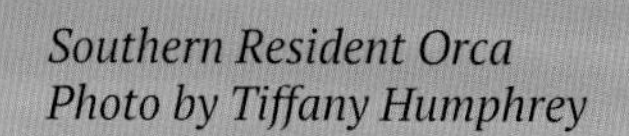

Southern Resident Orca
Photo by Tiffany Humphrey